***
A Noteworthy Americans &
Legends of the Plains
Quick Reader Book

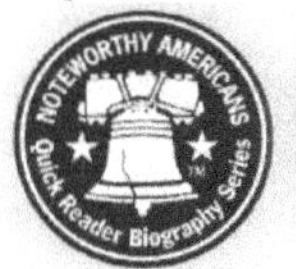

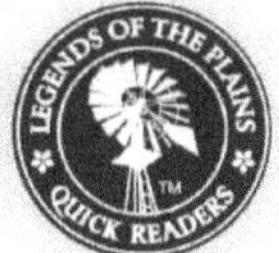

Secret Brother: The Story of Solon Borglum, "Sculptor of the Prairie"

by Jean A. Lukesh

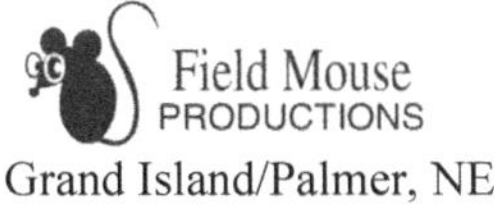

Grand Island/Palmer, NE

Published by Field Mouse Productions
Grand Island and Palmer, Nebraska

First Printed, 2015.
Printed in the United States of America.
Photos Courtesy of Cairo Roots Museum unless otherwise noted.
Artwork by Ron Lukesh.
The Noteworthy Americans and The Legends of the Plains Quick Reader series books were designed by Jean A. Lukesh (Ed.D., Curriculum & Instruction).

Lukesh, Jean A., 1950 -
Secret Brother: The Story of Solon Borglum, "Sculptor of the Prairie"

SUMMARY: A quick-reading biography of Solon Borglum—the lesser known and most often overlooked secret son of Danish Mormon immigrants who traveled the Mormon Trail to Utah in the 1860s, then changed their religion and lifestyle and moved to Nebraska. Despite his unusual childhood, Solon grew up to be a cowboy, rancher, sheriff, early Boy Scout leader, French World War I hero, Army art instructor, and the world famous artist nicknamed "The Sculptor of the Prairie." Solon's carving of at least one monumental-sized Plains Indian figure in the sandhills bluffs near his father's Central Nebraska ranch was the likely inspiration for his more famous older brother (John) Gutzon Borglum's sculpting of Mount Rushmore. (For 6th or 7th grade through adult readers.)

Noteworthy Americans Quick Reader Biography Series.
Legends of the Plains Quick Reader Biography Series.
1. Solon Borglum, 1868-1922—Biography. 2. Artists--Biography. 3. Sculptors—Biography. 4. World War I—Heroes. 5. Nebraska History. 6. France—World War I. 7. Solon Borglum, 1868-1922—Young Adult Biography.
I. Title. II. Subtitle. III. Series IV. Series
(YA) NB237.B62 .L85 978.2 (YA) B 920 [921]
ISBN 978-0-9888021-3-1

Cover Sculpture: Solon Borglum's *Bronco Buster* sculpture, also called *One in a Thousand*. (Photo courtesy, Buffalo Bill Center of the West, Cody Wyoming, U.S.A.; Gertrude Vanderbilt Whitney Trust Fund Purchase, 6.60.)

Dedication:

To the Borglums who carved out a new life in both the Old World and the New, especially to Solon's father James (Jens) Borglum, James's two wives (Ida and Christina), his seven children by Ida, and his two sometimes-secret but also loved sons by Christina: older brother (John) Gutzon Borglum, who later carved four faces of American presidents on Mount Rushmore in South Dakota, and most especially, the younger brother Solon Hannibal Borglum, "The Sculptor of the Prairie," who loved the Old West, Plains Indians, cowboys, and horses (as I do) and who carved Plains Indian faces and figures in the sandhills bluffs of Nebraska.

Also in loving memory of my long-gone and greatly missed horse Diamond who loved to swim rivers and lakes and to climb the bluffs at St. Michael (as did I!)—a place where Solon Borglum often rode as a cowboy and rancher, where he rested his own horse and looked down over the valley, and where he once carved huge Native American figures that later inspired his older brother Gutzon to carve other monuments on the land, as well.

And also in memory of taking part in an official, government-sanctioned and supervised archeological dig not far from White Cloud School and Cairo, Nebraska, just a few miles south of the former Borglum Ranch, during the summer of 1986. The resulting official documentation of that dig recorded the excavation of approximately two-thirds of one square (not round) pre- or proto-Pawnee earth lodge, cache pits/trash pits, arrowheads and points, a fish hook made from the ankle-bone of a pronghorn antelope, pieces of pottery and horn or bone tools, and some animal bones from a cooking pot, all dating back to pre-1300 A.D. After that excavation, artifact recovery, documentation, and aerial photography, that archeological site was then re-covered over with native soil.

Acknowledgements:

Thanks go to Solon Borglum's grandchildren David Borglum and Gwynneth Davies Kelley, and to Gwynneth's late mother and father who wrote the biography of Solon Borglum from which much of this book was drawn, *Solon Borglum: "A Man Who Stands Alone"*; to friends and facilitators Ken and Deb Harders, Jo Riedy, Walt Sorensen, Opal Schuett, and everyone with the Cairo Roots Museum—and to other local people: Lurlie Campbell, Val Vierk, and others of the surrounding area, including the Kemptar family for their stewardship and selfless use of their bluffs lands; to Tom and Twyla Witt, Gale Pemberton and Peggy Lang, Trish Beem, and others of the Highway 2 Scenic By-Way Group; my husband Ron, friend Tom, people at the Hall and Buffalo County Courthouses, friend and fellow historian E. A. Kral, friend/researcher Terri O'Brian, friends Mary Ann Carson (whose home is right alongside one branch of the Mormon Trail that runs to Murdock site near where her family lives), Renae Hunt of Stuhr Museum and Dave Scoggins and the Hall/Howard County Boy Scouts who made and/or facilitated the Mormon handcart trek to Murdock site in the spring of 2015; also park rangers Ed Menard and Zane Martin from the National Park Service; Audrey and Karl Shaff (authors of *Six Wars at One Time*); friends Ronnie O'Brien, Bill Peterson, Don Dingman, and others of OCTA; our Western Writers of America/OCTA friend and expert historian Will Bagley and Erick Wadsworth for their help with early Mormon and Mormon Trail details; and members of the LDS church and the Mormon Trails Organization for making genealogy and historical information available to researchers, historians, and genealogists; and to many more who gave time, interest, and support. Thank you, all!

Genealogy or Family Chart for the
James (Jens) Miller Haugaard de la Mothe Borglum family
and most secret son **Solon Borglum (the subject of this book)**

James (Jens) Miller Haugaard de la Mothe Borglum, 1839-1901

1st wife: Ida Mikkelsen/Michelsen, 1846?-1911

Children with 1st wife Ida:

James "Miller" Borglum (Junior), 1865-?

August Stanislaus Borglum, 1867-1952

Arnold Socrates Borglum, 1869-1932

Anna Christine Borglum, 1871-1939

Agnes Theodora "Dora" Ingeborg Borglum, 1876-?

Francis "Frank" Aloysius Borglum, 1879-1936

Harriet Maria Borglum, 1882-?

2nd wife: Christina Mikkelsen/Michelsen, 1847-?

Children with 2nd wife Christina; two sons,
sometimes called the "Secret Brothers":

John "Gutzon" Borglum, 1867-1941

Solon Hannibal Borglum, 1868-1922

Timeline of Important Events in the Life of Solon Borglum

1864 James & Ida Borglum, Danish Mormons on the Mormon Trail
1865 Ida's son Miller is born; Ida's sister Christina arrives from Denmark, James also marries Christina, according to Mormon Law
1867 On March 25, John Gutzon Borglum is born to Christina and James; in April, August Borglum is born to Ida and James
1868 Dec. 22, Solon Hannibal Borglum born to Christina and James
1869 Arnold is born to Ida; the Borglums change religion, move to Omaha, but fear persecution and prosecution
1871 Christina leaves family, as the Borglums move to St. Louis
1874 Borglum family moves back to Omaha, then Fremont, Nebraska
1883 James buys Nebraska ranch land; Family goes to California; Solon & Arnold work California ranch; Gutzon studies art in California
1884-5 Solon with family back in Omaha, planning Nebraska ranch
1885-93 Solon starts and runs Nebraska ranch on Loup River near Cairo
1887 Youngest half-brother Frank (8) is sent to the ranch to get well
1890 Gutzon visits ranch, tells Solon he should be an artist
1890-93 In between ranching, Solon takes some art classes in Omaha
1893 Gutzon visits Omaha; Solon goes to California with Gutzon
1895-97 Solon at Cincinnati Art Academy, then on to Paris
1898 Dec 10, Solon marries Emma Vignal of Paris, France
1899 Honeymoon on Crow Creek Reservation in South Dakota
1900 Solon wins many art awards in Paris; daughter Lilli is born
1901 Solon returns to America; wins many awards; son Paul is born
1902 Solon's wife and two children come to America from France
1903 Daughter Lilli dies; daughter Monica is born
1906 Solon buys Rocky Ranch at Silvermine, Connecticut
1911 Solon becomes Boy Scout leader at Silvermine; teaches art
1915 Death of friend Johnny Gruelle's daughter Marcella
1918-19 Solon with soldiers in France in World War I, receives French war medal; teaches A.E.F. soldiers how to sculpt in France
1922 Solon dies unexpectedly in Stamford, Connecticut
1925 Brother Gutzon begins carving Mount Rushmore, dies in 1941

Table of Contents

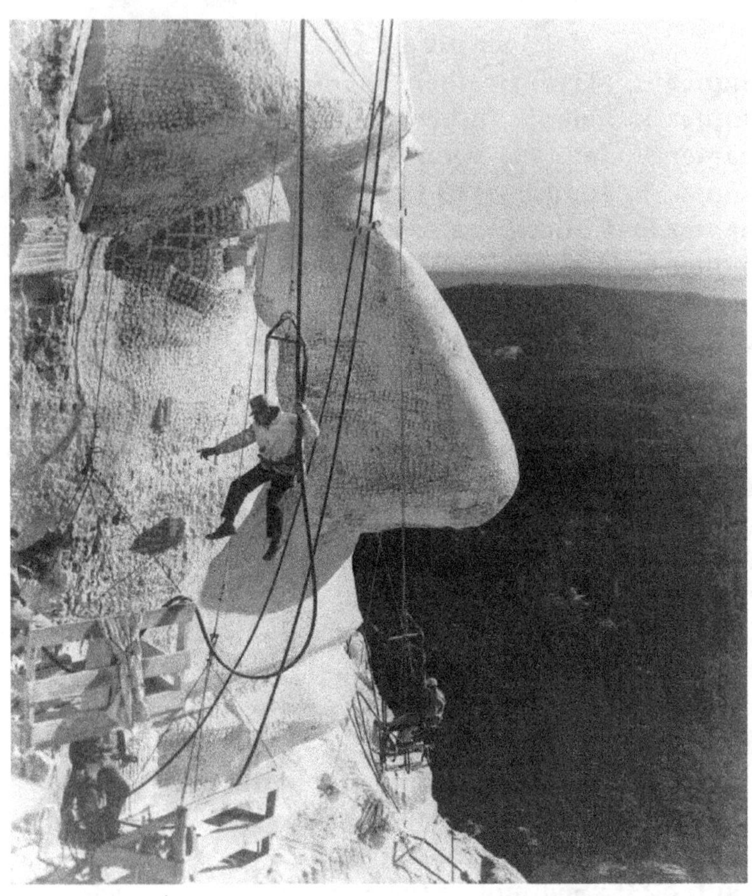

John Gutzon Borglum (Solon Borglum's older full-brother) on a swinging stage checking one of his monumental Mount Rushmore faces. (Photo courtesy, the National Parks Service.)

"Gutzon" may have been inspired to become a sculptor when he saw the Plains Indian figures his younger brother Solon had carved into a Nebraska bluff near their father's ranch many years earlier. But Gutzon did not start work on Mount Rushmore until after his brother Solon's death.

Gutzon and Solon were often mistaken for each other, because of their unusual names, their secret family history, their resemblance, their love of Old West art, and their "Borglum the Sculptor" shared nickname. But Solon was quieter and more easy-going, and he died younger. As a result, Solon was often the overlooked and forgotten one of the two secret brothers in their family.

Chapter 1:
Secret Brother: Solon Borglum

Today, Solon (SOL-un) Borglum's life is almost a secret. Hardly anyone knows who he was. If people recognize his name at all, they usually have him confused with his older, more famous brother John Gutzon (GUTZ-un) Borglum, the man who carved the faces of four American presidents on Mount Rushmore.

Younger brother Solon was also a great and famous artist. One of his titles was "The Sculptor of the Prairie." But he had nothing to do with Mount Rushmore—nothing, except that he inspired his older brother to become a sculptor and to use the face of the land as his canvas.[1]

Indeed, sculpting portraits into the hillsides was what Solon had done first—the carving of huge Native

American faces and figures in the sandhills bluffs near St. Michael, Nebraska, when Solon was in his late teens or early twenties. That was while he was living his dream of being a cowboy and running the family cattle ranch near there in the 1880s and early 1890s. That was before he became a world class artist himself and a war hero, and much more. But that is all part of that younger (and secret) brother Solon's story.

Long before that, in 1864, their father, James (or Jens) Borglum, a Danish Mormon immigrant, and his first wife Ida, came to America and traveled the Mormon Trail to Utah. There, James had two wives—that was a common practice among Mormons in those days, but it was illegal in most of the United States and its territories by 1862.[2]

But if James had not been a Mormon with two wives, his two most famous yet "secret" sons John Gutzon Borglum and Solon Hannibal Borglum might never have been born.

Years later, the Borglum family moved back to Nebraska. There, the children were told not to talk about their Mormon background, or their complex and unusual family structure, or why full-brothers John Gutzon and Solon were not always listed as family members with their seven half-brothers and half-sisters. But this book will talk about that, because it helps to understand Solon.

The first chapters of this book are the story of Solon's father—James (Jens) Borglum, his ancestors, his family, and how and why he came to America. That part is important because it helps set up the rest of the book for the story of James's most-secret son Solon Borglum who loved horses and Native Americans and being a cowboy and everything about the Old West.

So this is actually the story of Solon's family history, and of how and why Solon became a cowboy, a rancher, a sheriff, an award-winning artist called the "Sculptor of the Prairie," one of the first American Boy Scout leaders, a decorated World War I hero, an Army art instructor, and an inspiration to other artists, including his brother. In all ways, this is the story of Solon Borglum, that often-overlooked, nearly-forgotten, and sometimes secret younger brother of (John) Gutzon Borglum who carved Mount Rushmore.

Chapter 2:
Solon's Father and His Ancestors

A few years before the Civil War spread across America, a young unmarried man named Jens (Jenz) Borglum decided to change his life, his name, his religion, and his home country. He was not the first in his family to make lifestyle changes, and he would not be the last.[3] (His sons would make many changes of their own.)

In those days, that man's long and full name was kind of odd. It was Jens Møller (Mole-lur) Haugaard (Hah-guard) de la Mothe (day-luh Mothe) Borglum.

"De la Mothe" was a special title meaning "one of courage." That name was given to a knight who had saved the life of a prince during a hunting trip in 1190. That title was then passed down to that knight's sons and grandsons who lived in France and Denmark in Europe.[4]

In Denmark, that knight's family once lived in a village area named Borglum. In those days, Danish law required families to use the name of their village or monastery as their own last name.[5] So that knight's family also used the last name of Borglum.

Hundreds of years later, in 1864, when Jens Borglum decided to move to America, he would keep his two family names "de la Mothe" and Borglum. And he would pass those names down to his own six sons, including his two "secret sons" Gutzon and Solon.

Changing Religions

In 1190, that first Borglum knight and his family may have been Catholic. In Denmark, their family may have been Lutheran. But in the 1850s, several American missionaries brought the Mormon religion to Denmark and to many other European countries.

At that time, Jens Borglum's older sister Maren (Mare-en or "Mary") and her husband Hans Christian Hegsted became Mormon converts. So did Jens, and so did many of their family, friends, neighbors, and thousands of Danish and other European people—but not Jens and Maren's parents.[6]

For eight years, Jens worked hard in Denmark, learning the ways of the Mormon religion and converting others to it.[7] He was becoming a church leader.

Then war came to Denmark. The Mormon leaders did not want to lose their new people in war. They needed them in America, so that was where they sent them.

Changing Countries

Jens was eager to go to America at that time, but his sister Maren and her new family were not yet ready. Jens finally decided that his future could not wait, and he was soon on his way. Like many other immigrants, he would even change his first name to something more American. From that time on, he would call himself James instead of Jens.[8]

But James (or Jens) Borglum had much to learn about America. And in the 1860s, America was also a country at war. In fact, America was fighting two wars in the 1860s—The Civil War (or The War Between the States) in the Northern and Southern states in the East, and the Plains Indian Wars all across the Central Plains.

Chapter 3:
James Borglum Crosses the Ocean

In 1864, James (Jens) Borglum was a young man with many good qualities. People said he was intelligent, a student of the world, and a seeker of truth. They called him proud, independent, strong, healthy, idealistic, dedicated, and hard working. He was good with his hands and loved woodcarving, so he was a carpenter by trade.

He also had a dream. He planned to continue his work with the Mormon Church to become a Mormon leader in America. At that time, he was still unmarried and was the first in his family to go to the New World.[9]

On April 3, 1864, he started his great adventure when he left Copenhagen, the capital of Denmark, and took a ship across the cold North Sea to Germany. He turned 25 years old while on a train crossing Europe, then traveled by ship to Liverpool, England.[10] There, on April 27, he joined 973 other Danish Mormons and their American Mormon leader John Smith (nephew of the late Mormon leader Joseph Smith) at the boat docks.

Together, they all waited, with their personal items, clothing, bedding, and cooking pots, to board a big ship called *The Monarch of the Sea*. That ship would take them to the land of their dreams—America.[11]

Building Families

As large as that ship was, it was barely big enough for those nearly 1,000 Mormon passengers. Many of those people were unmarried strangers, but there would be little privacy onboard the ship. So something had to be done to make room for everyone and their belongings.

The Mormon solution was to pair up and marry as many single men and women together as possible.[12] Those couples could then combine their property and use less space. But after that pairing was done, there were still some single women left over.

Early Mormon law had an answer for that, too. Mormon men were allowed and encouraged to have more than one wife. They could even marry their wife's sisters as “sister-wives” to build large close-knit families.

Having more than one wife at the same time is sometimes called polygamy (po-LIG-uh-mee) or bigamy (big-uh-mee). A federal law in 1862 had made that practice illegal in parts of the United States. But having multiple wives was still a very common Mormon practice for many years.

Most of the new Mormons from Europe did not speak English. And they did not know America’s federal laws. So of course, they followed the laws and practices of their religion and their leaders.

Women’s Rights in the 1800s

At that same time, women all over the world generally had very little control over their own lives. They had almost no rights. They could not vote, and most of them had no money or property of their own.

Often their father or older brother decided almost everything of importance for them—even deciding who a girl would marry. After marriage, the husband usually decided the important things. Most younger women were not even supposed to travel anywhere without a husband, parent, brother, or older woman at their side.

So on April 27, 1864, many of those unmarried Mormon women on the docks at Liverpool allowed themselves to be paired up as first or second wives of the Mormon men there. Their new religion encouraged them to marry—even to marry a stranger who was already married. It was all part of what they had signed up to do. It was part of their new religion and their new lives.

James and Ida Borglum

On that day, James Borglum saw his neighbor Ida Mikkelsen (later spelled Michelsen). She was standing with her ten-year-old brother Lave (whose name was later changed to John). Ida was the oldest daughter of a Copenhagen furrier. She and her little brother would also be the first in their family to go to the New World. [13]

James and Ida knew each other, and they agreed to be man and wife. So that same day, they were married, along with other Mormon couples or trios in a big group ceremony.

The next day, they left Liverpool harbor on a ship called *The Monarch of the Sea*. Onboard were nearly 1,000 Mormon immigrants, who were all "leaving their homes, family, friends, language, country, and culture, in exchange for what they believed would be a better life."[14] They were bound for North America, to live with other Mormons in Salt Lake City in an area called Utah.

James and Ida's voyage on *The Monarch of the Sea* was relatively calm and lasted 36 days. Still, many people became ill along the way, and more than 40 people died on that ship while crossing the Atlantic Ocean. Most of those who died were just children.[15]

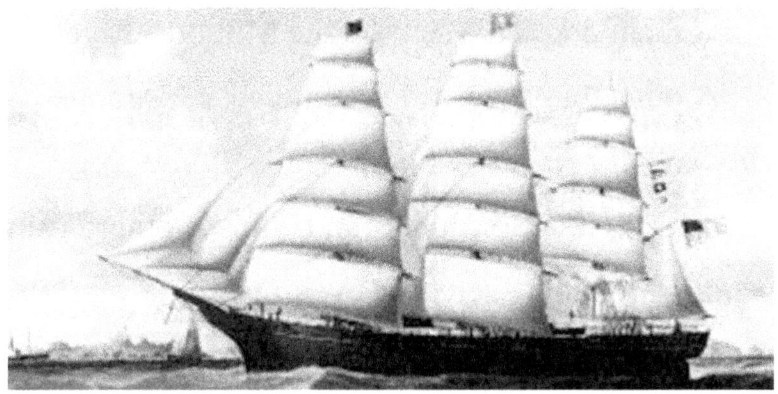

The Monarch of the Sea may have been the largest clipper ship to bring Mormon immigrants to America. Twice, it may have brought the most people—nearly 1,000 travelers in both 1861 and 1864. It was reportedly "an excellent vessel, large, roomy, and clean."[16] But still, more than 40 people died on the ship during that trip—more than one death per day. (Public domain image.)

It was called a clipper ship, because it had a sharp-edged body that sliced through the water like a knife and three large masts with several big sails that caught lots of wind. That made it sail across the ocean quickly at a steady clip, or as if clipping right along. In 1864, when James and Ida Borglum traveled on this ship to America, their journey lasted 36 days.

The Monarch of the Sea was reportedly lost at sea in 1880.[17]

Ships and Boats and Trains

After leaving *The Monarch of the Sea*, James and Ida Borglum, along with Ida's little brother and other Mormon immigrants from that ship, took a steamship up the Hudson River to Albany, New York. From there, they traveled by train, passing through the big cities of Rochester, Buffalo, Detroit, Chicago, and Quincy, on their way to St. Joseph, Missouri. At St. Joseph, they got on a riverboat and were sent up the Missouri River.[18]

Along the way, they entered a strange new world—a land at war, and a land at the edge of a wilderness. The Borglums and those other Danish Mormons probably were not even aware of where they were, or what was happening around them, or even what their new life would be like.

James and Ida's new life was just beginning. So was their journey—and so was their new family line.

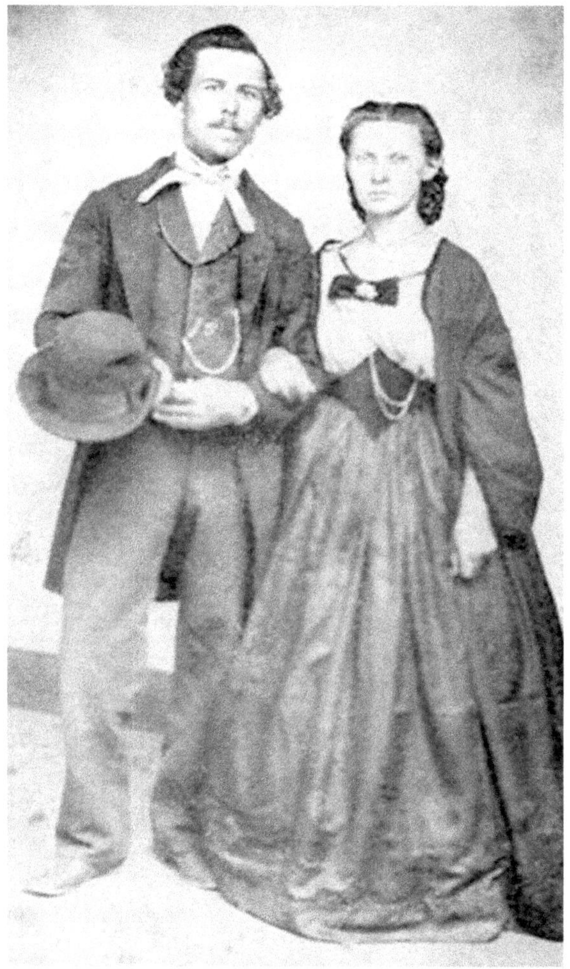

Newly-weds James (Jens) Borglum and 1st wife Ida Mikkelsen (later spelled Michelsen) in 1864. This couple came to America from Denmark as Mormons and married along the way. They would eventually have seven children of their own. (Photo courtesy, The Cairo Roots Museum Collection.)

In 1865, James followed Mormon custom and also married Ida's sister Christina who had just come from Denmark. James and 2nd wife Christina had two other sons—John Gutzon and Solon Hannibal Borglum.

A few years later, the Borglums left Utah and the Mormon faith. Then, James could no longer have two wives, so he could not claim Christina's sons. Later Christina left the family and left her two sons with their father. After that, James and his 1st wife Ida also raised Christina's two boys as their own.

Chapter 4:
Jumping-Off Points

The American Civil War was still going on in 1864 when James and Ida Borglum arrived in America. Reports say at least one Mormon riverboat was shot at by soldiers in that year.[19] Otherwise, riverboats were a good way to bring travelers west from St. Joseph, Missouri.

The paddle-wheelers traveled up the Missouri River and docked at whatever place was then the outfitting town or “jumping-off point” for westward travel along the overland trails. At such towns, people could buy supplies, wagons, livestock, and other things. There, travelers could find guides and could join other people heading across country. Such towns were the main starting points on the trails west.

But the Mormon jumping-off points and the

Mormon way of traveling in America had already changed a lot in the years before James and his first wife Ida came to America.

Winter Quarters, 1846-1847

When James Borglum first considered coming to America, he may have heard the history of the first Mormon jumping-off point called Winter Quarters. (Later that place became the town of Florence, near Omaha, in Nebraska Territory. Today, a Mormon museum and a big cemetery mark the trail site of those first Mormons to go west and the graves of hundreds of those Mormons who died there in that first year of 1846.)

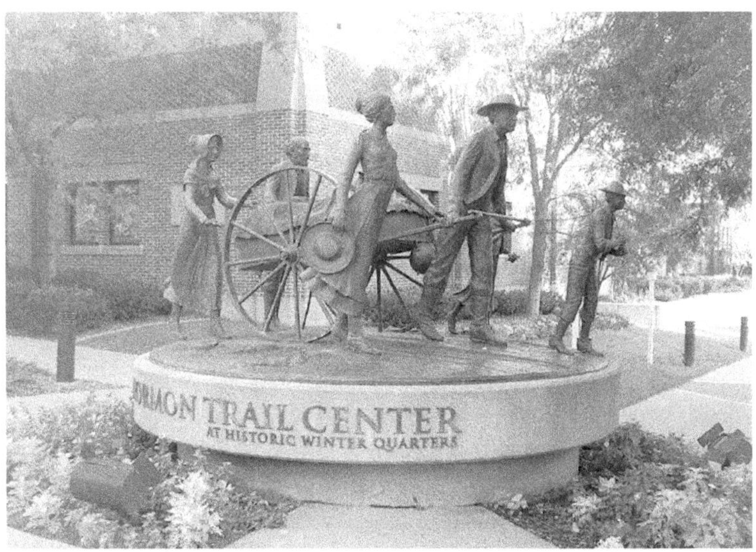

The Mormon Trail Center at Historic Winter Quarters, (Florence) Nebraska. Note the handcart being pulled by people, not animals.

Winter Quarters and Kanesville 1846-1859

From 1846 to 1847, Winter Quarters was the major jumping-off point or town for Mormons heading west from the Missouri River. But by 1848, the Mormons were having trouble with some nearby Plains Indians.

The Mormons then established a new jumping-off point just east of there, back across the Missouri River in Iowa. That new place, called Kanesville, became the major Mormon Trail jumping-off point until 1859 or 1860. Today Kanesville is called Council Bluffs, Iowa.[20]

At Kanesville, groups of Mormons rested, resupplied, and got ready to move west. When the time was right, they crossed the Missouri River and started out on the trail at Winter Quarters. From there, they walked west across Nebraska with covered wagons, or in the years between 1856 and 1860, they pulled handcarts loaded with their supplies and whatever they owned.[21]

Handcarts West

A handcart was a large two-wheeled cart or a small two-wheeled wagon that was made to be pulled by people, not animals. All the people had to walk. Over the next two to five months' time, those early Mormons walked about a thousand miles, pulling their handcarts loaded with food, supplies, and what little they owned. That was a very hard way for them to travel!

That original Mormon Trail ran along the north side of the Platte River. Other overland trails often ran along the south side of the river, or sometimes on both sides. The Mormons usually left later in the year than the wagon trains using the Oregon and California Trails. That was to avoid conflict with other travelers.[22] Mormon travelers also camped at their own rest stops along the trail on their way across country to Salt Lake City.

Nebraska City, 1860-1863

If James Borglum had come to America as a Mormon in the late 1850s, he would have pulled a handcart to Salt Lake City. But he was still a boy living in Denmark in those years. And by the time he came to America, things were changing along the Mormon Trail.

Around 1860, major political problems and serious health issues at Winter Quarters again caused Mormon leaders to make changes. They then began using other jumping-off points and other trails west, and another way of traveling, to get their people to Salt Lake City faster.

About that time, a man named Alexander Majors started using some western trails on the south side of the Platte River. Some of those trails started in Nebraska City, along the Missouri River (near Old Fort Kearny).

Majors was a partner in the freighting company of Russell, Majors, and Waddell (Wod-DELL). Their freight wagons took supplies on those more southerly overland routes called the Oxbow Trail, the Great Central Trail, or the Nebraska City Cut-off Trail that went to new Fort Kearny, Fort Laramie, and Salt Lake City. Mormon leaders soon saw the value of using those same freighting trails on the south side of the Platte River, too.

At the same time, Mormon leaders decided to stop using handcarts. Handcarts had always been slow moving and difficult to pull. They often broke down and needed repair, and most Mormon travelers could not buy and haul all the supplies they needed to take with them in those carts. Freight wagons seemed to be better vehicles for such a journey.

Down and Back Wagons

So in 1860, Mormon leaders in Utah developed a whole new system to finance, supply, and take their

Mormon people and goods west—and east too. They sent some of their men east, driving ox-drawn freight wagons full of goods and products to that new jumping-off point at Nebraska City. There the freighters could sell some goods and products while waiting for new Mormon immigrants to get off the riverboats and join them.

Those Mormon wagons were called "Down and Back Wagons" or "Down and Back Wagon Trains," because they took goods, supplies, and products both east to Nebraska City and west to Salt Lake City.[23] On the way back to Utah, Mormon freighters often served as suppliers, wagon masters, guides, and cooks for westward-heading Mormon travelers.

From 1860 through 1863, both freighters and Mormon travelers used those new trails and Nebraska City as their jumping-off place. By then, handcarts had become a thing of the past, but most Mormon travelers still had to walk more than a thousand miles, alongside the freight wagon trains all the way to Utah.

Agreements

Mormons travelers had to do other things, too. In exchange for supplies and services, Mormon travelers had to sign a contract. That contract said they agreed to follow Mormon laws and the orders of their wagon master, and to go all the way to Salt Lake City with the wagon train. They also agreed to stay with the Mormon Church and to repay what money they owed the church, plus 10% interest per year.[24] Those agreements were binding, but the trails were still changing.

Old Wyoming (Nebraska), 1864-1867

In 1864, the year James and Ida Borglum came to America, Alexander Majors started using another trail west. And the Mormons also began using that new trail.

The starting point for Majors' newest route was just a few miles north of Nebraska City. It started at the riverboat docks along the west side of the Missouri River, just east of the small town of Wyoming (or Old Wyoming) in eastern Nebraska Territory. That town was the new jumping-off point for many Mormons going west between 1864 and 1867, including the Borglums.[25]

After 1867, that whole way of traveling across country would change again, as new railroads, especially the Transcontinental Railroad called The Union Pacific, began to carry people and goods west.

Chapter 5:
Church Trains on the Mormon Trail

Today, the town of Wyoming (or Old Wyoming), Nebraska, no longer exists and is only listed on a few maps. But records say James and Ida Borglum landed there at the Missouri River boat docks in late spring of 1864. With them were Ida's little brother John and hundreds of other Mormons. The travelers then waited for the Down and Back Wagons to take them west.[26]

The Borglums and their companions were assigned to one Mormon wagon master, his crew, and several freight wagons. Their wagon master's name was Captain William B. Preston,[27] and his whole group was sometimes known as a Mormon "church train."[28]

On July 8, 1864, Captain Preston's wagon train left the town of Old Wyoming heading southwest. The

Borglums and almost 400 other Mormons walked beside the 200 oxen and 50 freight wagons hauling their personal goods and supplies.[29]

Those Mormons were lucky to be going west when they did. They were no longer required to pull handcarts. They had freight wagons and drivers with them to haul and provide food and goods, all the way from the Missouri River to Salt Lake City, Utah. The Mormon way of traveling had changed, but the people still had to walk that thousand mile trail.[30]

From Old Wyoming

Captain Preston's Church Train was probably the fourth Mormon wagon train to start out from Old Wyoming that summer of 1864. Over the next five weeks, ten more Mormon wagon trains and some other freight wagon trains followed. They would all be just days or weeks in front or behind each other on the trails.

During that spring and summer, nearly 2,500 people and 510 ox-drawn wagons started out from that small town.[31] Each wagon was usually pulled by four yoke of oxen, while other loose or tied livestock (horses, mules, oxen, cattle, and other animals) ran alongside.

The Trail Out of Old Wyoming Town

Like all the Nebraska City trails, that new trail from Old Wyoming town was on the south side of the Platte River. But just west of Old Wyoming, that trail took a different turn. It did not head north toward the Platte River like some trails did. It did not head straight west. Nor did it head southeast toward Nebraska City.

Instead, after leaving Old Wyoming, that new trail looped down toward the southwest. Then it connected with a branch of the Nebraska City Cut-off Trail, heading west. There were many advantages to that new route.

Advantages of the Old Wyoming Trail

By using that combination of Old Wyoming trail and Nebraska City Cut-off Trail, Captain Preston and other Mormons and freighters were able to avoid a lot of problems. That route took them away from some of the boggy spots near the Platte River. It also avoided bigger towns and heavier traffic near the Missouri River. It even by-passed much of the traffic going into and coming out of Nebraska City. That route also stayed away from many of the non-Mormon wagon trains and freight trains heading west on branches of the California Trail.

There were other advantages to using that new trail, too. It was almost always on dry and solid ground, and it was usually within a mile of good grass and water.[32] And when that trail turned west, it ran almost straight west for most of the way to new Fort Kearny (south of the town of Kearney, Nebraska) along the Platte River. As a result, that new trail from Old Wyoming to new Fort Kearny was 40 miles shorter than many of the old trails—and in those days, 40 miles was two days' travel by ox-drawn wagon or foot.[33]

Branches of Many Trails

Travelers heading west in the mid-1800s along the many branches of the Mormon, Oregon, California, and other Trails did not follow directly in each other's footsteps. But they often used parts of the same trails and some of the same river crossings. They also used whatever resources they could find (fresh grass for the animals; firewood, cow chips, or dry grass for the fire; wild game animals for food; and other such resources).

With so many people and animals on those trails, travelers quickly used up most of the natural resources. Without meaning to do so, they ate, trampled, or destroyed many of the plants. That left very little for others who came later. They also dirtied the water and passed along some diseases. Because of that, trail routes sometimes were changed and road ranches were needed.

Road Ranches

A road ranche (usually spelled ranche instead of ranch) was a farm, a small ranch, a little settlement, or a store along the trail, where travelers could get safe water and buy basic foods like beans and flour. Some road ranches even became post offices, Pony Express stops, stage stations, or later railroad stations or towns.

At some road ranches, travelers could rest; trade worn-out livestock for fresh animals; get shoes put on their horses, mules, or oxen; or have their wagons repaired. (Road ranches were somewhat like today's truck stops and convenience stores.)

Because Mormon beliefs and customs were often very different than those of other travelers, Mormons were not always welcome at some towns and road ranches. To avoid trouble, the Mormons often stayed on their own trails and had their own road ranches and camping spots.

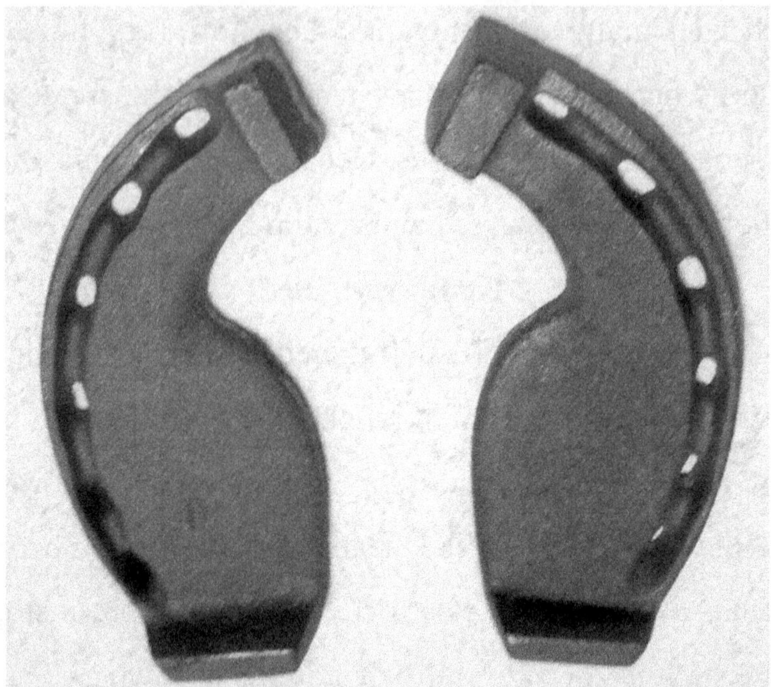

A pair of matched ox shoes for one hoof. (From the author's collection.) On long journeys, oxen (steers or male cattle that were used to pull wagons or plows) needed shoes to protect their hooves, like horses and mules did. But cattle have split hooves, so one ox needed four pair (or eight matched pieces) of ox shoes on its hooves. Travelers could sometimes have ox shoes or horseshoes put on their animals at road ranches along the trails. Compare one matched pair of ox shoes to one horseshoe or muleshoe.

Rules on the Trail

The rules of the trail and a code of behavior needed to be very strict for such a long journey. So a wagon master's word was law. He had the power to christen, marry, bury, punish, banish, or hurry his people along.

There was little comfort, health care, or cleanliness

on the trail. Travelers generally walked all day long. At night, if room allowed, women might bed down in or under the wagons. Men often slept outdoors by the campfires. They lived that way for months in all kinds of weather, until they reached the end of their journey. Travel was slow and difficult, but travelers had no time to waste and could not wait long for anyone too slow or too ill to keep up.

Some people died along the way. The dead were often buried beside, or sometimes right on, the trail. Then the graves were walked on, to pack down the dirt and hide the burial. That helped keep animals from digging up the bodies. Few trail graves were marked, and only a few of those markers have survived.

For their own survival, travelers knew they had to cross the plains and get through the mountains to safety before winter hit—or everyone on their wagon train could die. Those people who survived, generally did so by following the strict orders of very experienced leaders.

Chapter 6:
Across Nebraska to the Great Salt Lake

Despite the hurry west, James Borglum must have liked the look of Nebraska Territory. At that time, he was committed to the Mormon way of life. He was heading to Salt Lake City in Utah. (But a few years later, he would change his mind and bring his family back to Nebraska.)

With Preston's wagon train, the Borglums traveled the Nebraska City Cut-off Trail (or Fort Kearny Cut-off Trail) south of the Platte River.[34] They may have passed far south of Murdock Site (near today's Doniphan, Nebraska), then they traveled another 40 or more miles west until they came to Fort Kearny Crossing, two miles west of that fort. That was near Ben Holladay's stage stop. Mormon journals say the Platte River was sometimes a mile wide and very deep not far from there.[35]

The Preston wagon train probably turned north at that Fort Kearny Crossing and forded the Platte River. North of the river, the wagon train joined the old Mormon Trail and headed west again to Utah.

Plains Indian Lands

In those days, the Nebraska plains seemed to be nothing but wilderness, even though that area was peopled by several Plains Indians tribes. Most travelers on the trails could not tell one tribe from another. Newcomers may have feared the Plains Indians, but they seldom considered that the land ever belonged to them.

The Pawnee

By the 1860s, the relatively friendly Pawnee Indians were in a very bad way. At one time, they had been the most numerous tribe in Nebraska Territory. They had claimed or hunted a major portion of that area. But by the mid-1800s, thousands of their people had died from plains warfare and from the diseases on the trails.

By then, the Pawnee had sold off most of their former lands to the government, even though they had no understanding of what it meant to sell their lands. Then they had been pushed further north, away from their former villages, farms, and hunting grounds, and their major meat supply—the buffalo herds. The Pawnee were then moved further away from the trails, to a small Indian reservation (now called Nance County, Nebraska).

Life on that reservation was very foreign to the Pawnee way of life. They had no understanding of why they had to change their ways and follow the rules of people who did not understand them.

The Pawnee were great farmers and hunters, but their people were dying on the reservation. Generally friendly to white people, they were also very curious, independent, and resourceful. So some of them returned to their former lands to beg for food or to collect loose livestock from wagon trains. That caused problems. Many wagon travelers wrote in their journals that the Pawnee were beggars, thieves, and a nuisance. Travelers did not know how much the Pawnee world had changed.

Hostile Plains Indians

By the 1860s, the most powerful Plains Indians along the trails were the Lakota (sometimes called the Sioux) and their Cheyenne and Arapaho friends. They were angry about travelers crossing their hunting lands.

At the same time, many of the soldiers who were stationed at the western forts were sent back East to fight in the Civil War that was still going on in the eastern states. That left the forts, towns, road ranches, wagon trains, travelers, and other people unprotected for hundreds of miles on and around the trails.

Those Plains Indians soon realized that many of the soldiers were gone from the forts. Some of the more hostile tribes, especially the Lakota, Cheyenne, and Arapaho then took that opportunity to try to stop the wagon people from crossing their hunting lands. The western trails of Nebraska, Kansas, and neighboring territories became Plains Indian war zones in the 1860s.

Other Dangers

Plains warfare on those trails was often more common in those years. But there were other dangers as well—such as accidents, illness and disease, wild animals, bad weather, dangerous river crossings, quicksand, and even cultural clashes with other people.

The Borglums and Captain Preston's wagon train had some of those problems. But they kept going west. They reached Salt Lake City in September of 1864.

Chapter 7:
The Borglum Family Doubles

James and Ida Borglum were very lucky. They reached the end of the Mormon Trail safely. They were eager to start their new way of life in Salt Lake City.

But it would not be an easy life. They had little or no money. They were learning English, but they did not understand American laws or culture, or why the Mormons lived away from other Americans. And they did not really know what life would be like for them in their new and promised land of Utah.

At that time in 1864, Salt Lake City was already crowded with Mormons from America, England, Sweden, Denmark, Norway, Germany, and other countries. No one could expect special treatment, not even men like James Borglum who had been working for eight years in Denmark to become a Mormon elder.[36]

Mormon leaders demanded strict obedience, dedication, and hard work from their people. The Borglums would have to continue to work hard just to try to fit into that new American religious community, and to survive, especially with winter coming.

Salt Lake City

In Salt Lake City, James Borglum found part-time work as a carpenter and as a sawyer or sawmill worker. He rented two small rooms in someone else's house and moved his wife Ida and her little brother into their new home. They were glad to have a place to live. That first winter was bitterly cold.

The following spring, Ida's first child was born. They named him James Miller Haugaard de la Mothe Borglum (Junior) after his father. Miller, as he was called, may have been the first Borglum born in America.

Ida and James sent letters back to their relatives in Denmark, telling them about the baby and describing their travels and their Mormon way of life in America.

New Arrivals

Before long, James's sister Maren, her husband

Hans Christian Hegsted, and their baby son Vincent Charles Hegsted also came to America. The Hegsteds came to Utah with a Mormon wagon train led by Captain Miner G. Atwood. But the Hegsteds did not come alone. They also brought Christina (or Christiane) Mikkelsen. She was the younger, unmarried sister of James's wife, Ida (Mikkelsen) Michelsen Borglum.[37]

The overland journey to Salt Lake had not been easy for Maren, her husband, their new baby, and Christina. First, their ship almost sank during a storm at sea. Then, on the trail, their wagon train was attacked by hostile Plains Indians who killed some of the men and took one woman captive. After that, an early snowstorm trapped their wagon train in the mountains.[38]

So many bad things happened to them along the way that it took them two months longer to reach Utah than it had taken James and Ida. The Hegsteds did not even reach Salt Lake until early November 1865.[39]

Close Quarters

By that time, the four Danish newcomers could find no place to stay in the city. With winter on its way, the Hegsteds and Christina had no choice but to move in with their Borglum family in their two small rooms. There, the crowding became almost unbearable.

James, Ida, their infant son Miller, and Ida's little brother John could all crowd into one of the rooms. Then Maren, her husband Hans, and their infant son could live in the other. But that still left no privacy, and no proper place, for Ida's sister Christina—an 18- or 19-year-old single woman—with nowhere else to live.

What To Do With Christina?

Mormon leaders frowned on an unmarried young woman living in a crowded house with two men who were not her father or brother. They felt the proper thing to do was to find Christina a husband and get her married right away. But she did not want to marry a stranger and did not want to move away from her family.

As before, the Mormon Church had an answer, and Christina was already living with it. According to Mormon law, she would also marry James Borglum—her sister's husband—and become his second wife (or sister-wife). In that way, Christina could also help raise her own little brother, her sister's children, and also her own children when they were born.

The church had decided Christina's future for her. She may not have been happy with that decision, but there was nothing she could do about it.

Two Wives, Too Crowded

Still wanting to do well in the Mormon faith, James agreed to that arrangement. Two weeks later, James and Christina were married in the Mormon Church.[40] James then had two sister-wives—Ida and Christina. According to Mormon law, that made their living arrangement proper. But that did little to help the family's crowded conditions. And those conditions would soon get much worse and more difficult.

Chapter 8:
New Homes and Baby Boys

The leaders of the Mormon Church in Salt Lake City were looking for Mormon families to start a new settlement in Idaho, just across the Utah border. They told James to take his family and travel north with another Mormon wagon train to that new area.

Unhappy with the crowding in the city and thinking that things might be better in a new place, James agreed to the move. His family joined the wagon train and made the journey to Bear Lake near Ovid, Idaho. There, he claimed land for a farm and built his family a two-room log cabin.[41]

But things soon went from bad to worse in that cabin in Idaho. The following summer was too short and too chilly to grow good crops, and then the next winter and early spring were both bitterly cold. Grasshoppers ate what few crops could be raised, and hostile Indians threatened the safety of the settlers.[42]

Maren and her Hegsted family had stayed in Salt Lake City, but even so, conditions did not improve at the Borglums' new cabin at Bear Lake, near Ovid, Idaho. Tempers were short there in the wilderness. And the cabin was still over-crowded with James, his first wife Ida, their baby Miller, James's second wife Christina, and probably the women's little brother John.

More and More Crowded

During that time, the Borglum cabin became even more crowded. That was when both of James's wives had new babies within a month of each other. Second-wife Christina had her first child then, a son named John Gutzon Borglum, near Bear Lake, Idaho, on March 17, 1867. (Gutzon was another Borglum family name.)

Then just a month later, Christina's older sister Ida (James's first wife) gave birth to her second son, August Stanislaus (STAN-iss-sloss) Borglum. James then had three young sons, all with impressive-sounding names. That trend would continue, and so would the crowding.

Unhappiness

In Denmark, Ida and Christina had lived together with their family in a house in a big city. In Salt Lake City, the two sister-wives had not gotten along well in their rented rooms. In their two-room wilderness cabin in Idaho, they lived in even more difficult conditions.

They were city people who knew nothing about farming. The two sister-wives were unhappy with the hard work, the lack of food, the discomfort, the crowding, the bad weather, the isolation of living in the wilderness, the threat of hostile Indians, and the strictness of Mormon life. The women argued bitterly and often.

No one in the family was happy, not even James, who soon realized that his dream of becoming a church leader was not going to come true. He knew he had to make some changes. But he did not know what to do.

Opportunities in Ogden

Then one day, James heard that a transcontinental railroad was being built through the new and growing town of Ogden, Utah, just north of Salt Lake City. That meant there would be jobs available there, and Ogden was less strict and less Mormon than Salt Lake City.

James decided to go to Ogden to look around. But he knew he could not take his whole family with him. Where would they all stay and how could he afford to feed them there? He decided to leave his first wife and family at Bear Lake and just take his second-wife Christina and her baby (John Gutzon) with him to Ogden.

There, James found the conditions to be so much more comfortable, that he rented a house in Ogden and lived there with Christina and her new baby. He even found a good-paying job with the railroad. He worked hard and made a good name for himself.

Still, he knew he could not just leave the rest of his family at Bear Lake. Both of his wives would soon have new babies again, and both of them needed him.

Difficult Decisions

But his time in Ogden taught James something very important. By then, he knew he was never going to be a Mormon leader. He also knew he did not want to go back to living in the strict Mormon ways, and he did not want to live as a husband with two wives out in the wilderness again. His wives did not want that either.

But that raised new problems—he still had two

homes in two different places, two wives, and two sets of children. And polygamy was illegal in most of America, even in parts of Utah. James thought about what to do with his life and what to do with his growing family.

He was not a man who could run away from his problems. He could not abandon his family. He was responsible for them. He had to do something. But what?

Responsibilities

While he searched for answers, James continued working at his railroad job. When he had enough money, he paid off what he owed the Mormons. Then he sold his Bear Lake cabin and moved his whole family to Ogden.

There in Ogden, both of his wives soon had their next new baby sons. On December 22, 1868, James's second-wife Christina gave birth to her second (and last) son with her husband James. They named that baby Solon Hannibal Borglum.[43] (Solon is the real subject of this book.) Solon was a full brother to John Gutzon Borglum—and a half-brother to Ida's sons.

Six months later, James's first wife Ida had her third son, Arnold Socrates (SOK-ruh-teez). Solon and Arnold were half-brothers. They would be best friends.[44]

Chapter 9:
Coming Apart

By the time half-brothers Solon and Arnold were born, James's two wives no longer got along. They argued bitterly. That made things uncomfortable for everyone. No one was happy with their three-way marriage, lifestyle, and religion.

By then, Ida and Christina's parents had also moved to America. They had traveled to Omaha and decided to stay there. (Nebraska had been a territory when James and his first wife Ida crossed the plains on the Mormon Trail in 1864, but that territory had become the state of Nebraska on March 1, 1867, not long before Christina's first baby, John Gutzon, was born.)

Omaha was one of the central starting points for the Union Pacific Railroad. James worked for that same railroad in Utah. Omaha was a growing town, and with family there, it seemed like a good place for the whole Borglum family to live. James and his wives decided to leave the Mormon Church and Utah, and move to Omaha. But that would not solve all their problems.

Moving to Nebraska

In 1870, James settled his debts in Utah and booked railroad tickets to Omaha, for himself, his two wives, their five young sons, and probably for Ida's little brother.

It must have felt odd, riding across country in a train that ran so close to the Mormon Trail, a trail that James and Ida had once walked while going west. But Omaha was not a Mormon area, and federal laws said it was illegal for a man—even a Mormon—to have two wives. By that time, federal marshals were even arresting Mormons in Utah for having more than one wife.[45]

It may have felt good to James, to leave the strictness of his old way of life, but he and both his wives would have to make even more changes if they wanted to be accepted—and not arrested—in Omaha or elsewhere. They would have to change their family and their lives.

Restructuring the Family

At that time, James and his second wife Christina may have had their marriage "unsealed" under Mormon law. (That is a Mormon term used for when a husband and wife divorce each other.) Even divorced, they still had to hide the fact that James had ever had two wives and two sets of children, or he could have been arrested.

Christina and her children were still with the family, so James had to come up with a new family arrangement to help keep his secret. Somehow, it was decided that James and Ida would live together in a house in Omaha as husband and wife, with their own three sons. (James and Ida would later have other children too.)

At the same time, James's second wife Christina would live with the family in that same house, but not as a wife. Instead, she would be listed on the government census records as a housekeeper, and she would use her Americanized maiden name of Michelsen not Borglum.[46]

Secret Sons

On the 1870 Omaha census, Christina's two boys John Gutzon and Solon were correctly listed as Christina's sons. But the census did not give their father's name or Christina's husband's name. In that way, John Gutzon and Solon became James Borglum's two secret sons. James felt he could not risk using his own name on the records and being arrested, even though having two wives had once been an acceptable part of his religion.

That must have been an especially difficult and awkward way for Christina and her two sons to live—with the family—but not really a part of it. The children were all very close, so that must have been very uncomfortable and difficult for all of them.

A New Way of Life

At the same time, James also had to find a way to make a living so he could feed and care for his growing family. He still enjoyed woodcarving and carpentry, but there was not much call for that in Nebraska.

Fortunately, one of his new friends was a doctor in Omaha. He saw that James was good with his hands and encouraged him to become a doctor, too. With his friend's help, James prepared for medical school and was then admitted to a medical college in St. Louis, Missouri.

Christina Leaves the Family

In 1871, while the Borglums were packing to

move to Missouri, Christina saw a chance to make a new life for herself, too. One day, she kissed her sons Johnnie and Solon goodbye. Then she took her few belongings and left her boys to be raised by James and Ida.

Aunt Tina, as Christina was called after that, then moved in with her own parents in Omaha. From then on, she had little, or nothing, to do with her own two sons or with James's other children.[47]

No one really knows why Christina left that way. Perhaps she just wanted to make a clean start for herself. Maybe she felt she had been forced into marriage too soon. Or maybe she just thought James and Ida could give her boys much more than she could at that time.

James may even have encouraged Christina to leave the family and to let him take her boys. That may have made it easier for Christina, too. She was a young woman with no money and no way to make a living for her children. But by herself, she could start a new life.

After a while, she even moved away from her parents, remarried, and had another family of her own. (So Solon and John Gutzon eventually had other siblings that they never knew.)

First-wife Ida then raised all nine of James's children as brothers and sisters—Ida's own seven children and also her sister Christina's two sons, John Gutzon and Solon.

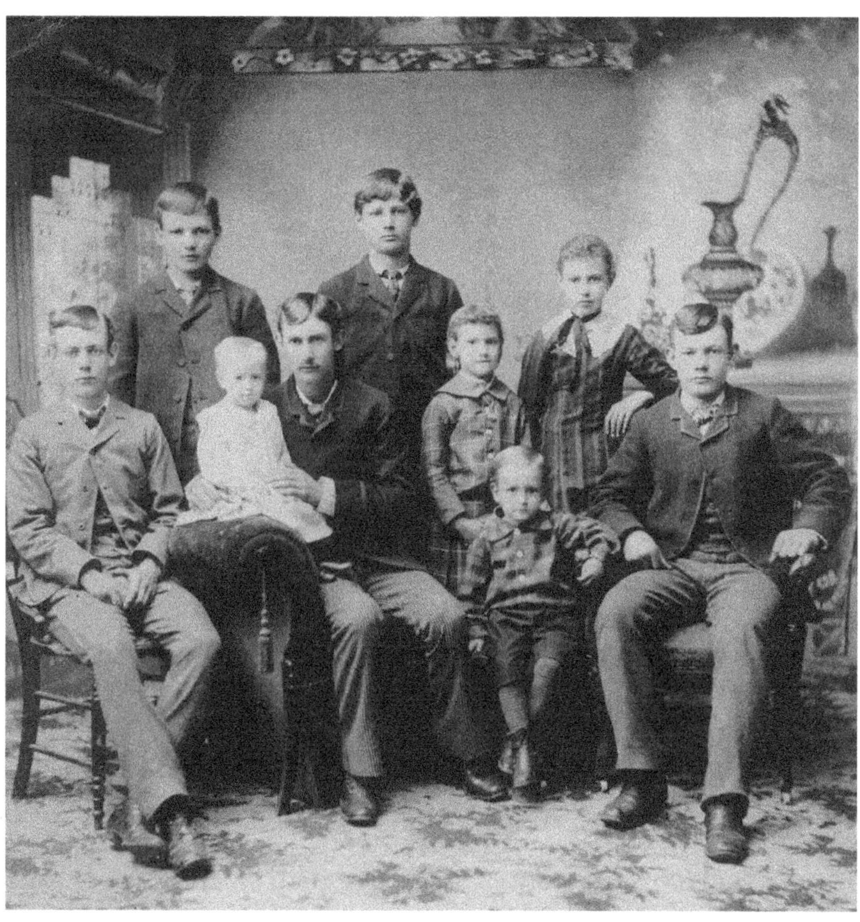

James Borglum's children (Christina's two children and Ida's seven), 1880, from left to right: August, Solon (Christina's second son), baby Harriet, Miller, Arnold, Theodora ("Dora"), little brother Francis ("Frank"), oldest sister Anna, and John Gutzon ("Gutzon" or Johnnie; Christina's first son). (Photo courtesy of Solon H. Borglum and Borglum family papers, Archives of American Art, Smithsonian Institution; photographer unidentified.)

Chapter 10:
House Calls and Schooling

Little is known about the Borglums' time in St. Louis, but in 1874, Dr. James Borglum finished medical school. He moved his big family back to Omaha to practice medicine there, but before long, he and a doctor friend traded offices. Then James moved his family to the nearby town of Fremont, northwest of Omaha.

Fremont was a wild place in those days, and Doctor Borglum stayed busy patching up cowboys who had knife or gunshot wounds or horse and cattle-related injuries. He also tended some of the nearby Plains Indians, as well. Sometimes he even stayed out in the country overnight at ranch houses or in tipis (teepees).

Road Trips

The doctor owned several horses, and his sons

(especially Christina's boys, Gutzon and Solon) often took turns driving his horse and buggy for him, so he could doctor someone and then sleep on the way home. But none of the doctor's boys enjoyed that horse handling job more than James's son Solon did.

Solon loved horses. He idolized the Plains Indians and dreamed of being a cowboy.[48] To him, it was a treat and an adventure to go out in the country, even if his father took that time to lecture to him about schoolwork.

Those trips gave Solon a chance to study the way horses, cowboys, and Native Americans looked and moved, so he often did some sketching while he waited for his father to finish doctoring someone. And sometimes he even took part in the doctoring as well.

Changing Religion Again

In Omaha and Fremont, the Borglum family joined the Catholic Church.[49] James and Ida still worried that someone would find out their secret, so they did what they could to hide the fact they had ever been Mormon.

There was nothing wrong with being Mormon, but they did not want anyone to find out James had had two wives and two sets of children at the same time. The

Borglums knew that the law against that could still destroy their family and send James to jail.

Secrets

It was no secret that James had a lot of children, and people often noticed that August, Gutzon, Solon, and Arnold were especially close in age. It did not help that Gutzon was very vocal about how he missed his real mother. People were very curious about all of that.

By then, most of the Borglum children had been too young to remember much about their Mormon way of life—and the family was not allowed to talk about it. James told his family that "The world…does not need [to know] the particulars of our life. It is not their business." So when anyone asked them questions, the children usually followed their father's orders and changed the subject quickly.[50] But questions did not always go away.

Missing Mom

Solon Borglum had only been about three, and his brother Gutzon had been close to five when their real mother Christina left the family. Both brothers missed their mom, but younger brother Solon had not known her nearly as well or as long as his older brother Gutzon had.

That may have made it easier for Solon to accept his Aunt Ida as his stepmother, and that probably helped him fit in better with his father and the rest of the family. It also helped that Solon was often quiet and agreeable, good-natured and adaptable, with a calm inner strength and a great spirit of independence and adventure.

Solon's older brother Gutzon loved his family, as well, but he had a very different personality and temperament. He too had a lot of inner strength, and he was very independent. But he was also outspoken, self-centered, a bit willful, and very angry. And he often had trouble dealing with the fact that his real mother had left him.

Gutzon's Anger Mis-Management

Gutzon did not understand why his mom had left him. He took it personally. He even made up stories to help him accept the situation and make it seem more acceptable to himself. Sometimes he told people that his real mother, Christina, had been his father's first wife (not his second). He told people that she had died, and that after that, his heartbroken father had married her sister Ida.[51]

But in his own heart, Gutzon knew that his mother was alive and that she had left him. Or maybe he thought she had been forced away from the family. He may even have blamed his father. Angry and rebellious, Gutzon often ran away from home and went looking for his mother. (Solon would have liked to have gone along, too, but mostly just for the adventure.) Gutzon never found his mother, and he sometimes had to be brought back to his father's house by force.[52]

Schooling for Gutzon and August

Maybe James grew tired of Gutzon running away from home. Or maybe he just wanted his children to learn more about the Catholic religion. In any case, James sent Gutzon and his half-brother August away to a boarding school at St. Mary's, Kansas, when they were teenagers.

As odd as it may sound, being sent away from the family may have been the best thing that could have happened to Gutzon. He was not at St. Mary's long when a teacher there helped him develop a strong interest in what would become his life's work—art.[53]

Another teacher there also helped Gutzon's half-brother August find his own passion for what would become his life's work—music. Before the end of that school year, both older boys would be well started on the road to their adult careers in the arts.

Schooling for Solon

Younger brother Solon's schooling was different. Solon was an intelligent boy, but his busy family had moved often, so he had missed out on a lot of schooling. As a boy, he did not care about grades. Instead, he preferred to miss as much school as he could. Later, he would regret his lack of education.[54]

In the 1800s and early 1900s, many children were not required to go to school beyond the 8th grade. They were needed on farms and in factories, so they often quit school and went to work at adult jobs early in life.

In 1883, Solon finished one very successful school year at Creighton College's Preparatory School in Omaha. He planned to return to Creighton the next year. But things changed, and he did not go back.

By then, the whole Borglum family had come down with "California Fever," and they would move west again. There, Solon would discover what he thought would become his own life's work—being a cowboy.

Chapter 11:
"California Fever"

In late 1882 or early 1883, oldest brother Miller Borglum probably finished his own last year of school in Omaha. Miller was about eighteen years old, and he may have been the first in his family to come down with "California Fever" or "Gold Coast Fever."

That did not mean Miller was sick. He was just excited by all the wonderful stories he heard about California, and how people were getting rich out there.

Miller decided to go to California to see for himself. In those days, it was common for a strong, healthy young man to leave home at an early age, to try to make his way in the world. Miller thought he was old enough, so he either left on his own or convinced his whole family to go west with him.

Moving to California

In Los Angeles, Miller got a job driving a horse and buggy around town for one of America's most influential women writers of the time. Her name was Helen Hunt Jackson. She would become famous for her book *Ramona*, a novel about the mistreatment of California's Native American people.

Miller's younger half-brother John Gutzon also went to California at that time. There, Gutzon worked for an artist making wood block art prints. But before long, Gutzon got a job painting art murals on buildings. Then he decided to go to art school.

But California Fever had also spread to their father James and to the other Borglums. In 1883, the whole Borglum family moved from Nebraska to that rapidly growing city of Los Angeles, California.

Ranch Land

Somewhere along the way to California, Dr. James Borglum may have bought ranch land in both Nebraska and California. Land records show that on October 8, 1883, James paid the Union Pacific Railroad $960 for 640 acres (or 1 square mile) of unbroken land close to the

Loup River and Sweet Creek in Hall County, Nebraska.[55]

James had once worked for the Union Pacific and may have heard that a new railroad would soon be coming to that area. Or perhaps he saw an advertisement about Hall County railroad land for sale while at one of the train stations on his way to California. Either way, he probably hoped to make a profit with that land.

Around that same time, James also became involved in a cattle and horse ranch north of Los Angeles. It was in a beautiful area of mountains and valleys.

The idea of living on that ranch in California made James's once-secret-son Solon happy, and Solon soon decided to go live on the ranch away from his family.

Solon's Dream of Being a Cowboy

Solon and his younger half-brother Arnold were close in age. They were best friends and went everywhere together. People even called them "the twins."

Solon was only about 5'6" tall. He was smaller than Arnold, but he was tough. Arnold always said that Solon was much stronger than he looked and could have wrestled down a man twice his size, but Solon was never mean. He just would not allow anyone to be bullied.[56]

Solon treated everyone fairly and with respect. Both he and Arnold were very good tempered and made friends wherever they went.

Solon had always loved horses. He would never outgrow that love, and he wanted to be a cowboy. When he wasn't riding horses, he was drawing pictures of horses or cowboys. Horses, his art, and the cowboy way of life were the things he loved most at that time. He also loved being outdoors. So Solon decided that he and Arnold should become full-time cowboys on their dad's California ranch. (The rest of the family lived in town.)

Arnold went along with that idea, and the two teens convinced their dad that cowboying was what they wanted to do with their lives. Their father James decided to let them try. He probably thought they would get tired of all the hard work—but Solon never did.

California Cowboy

Solon absolutely loved that California cowboy life—the more dangerous and difficult and outdoorsy it was, the more he loved it. Discomfort and physical injuries seldom stopped him from anything.

Years before, while working with some horses in

Fremont, he had been kicked in the head by a wild mustang. He would bear a small scar of that curved hoofprint on his forehead for the rest of his life—but such injuries would never stop him from working with horses.[57] Being a cowboy was Solon's dream come true.

Solon loved being a cowboy, but his half-brother Arnold did not care much for being outdoors or for horses or cattle. Still, Arnold loved his brother Solon and went along with the idea for a while. The two of them lived and worked hard on that California ranch, seldom seeing the rest of the family.

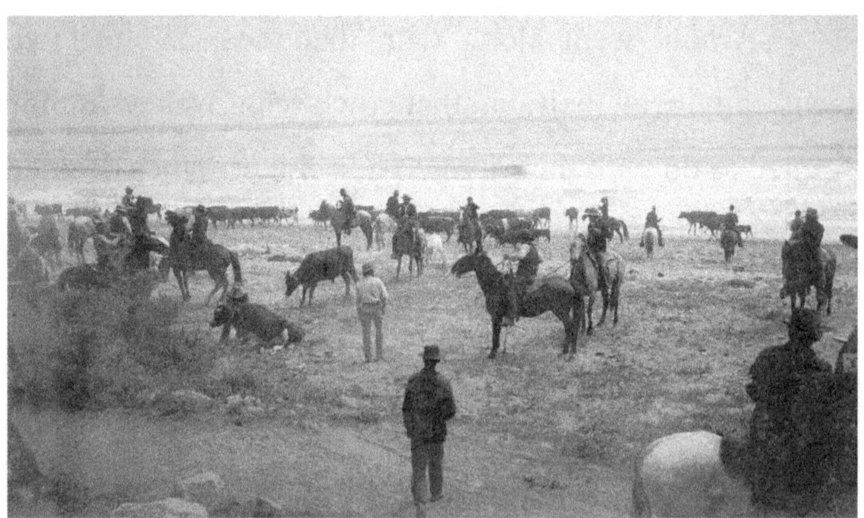

Cowboys at work on the Borglum Ranch in California, 1883-1884. Solon was reportedly one of the cowboys on horseback. (Photo courtesy, Solon H. Borglum and Borglum family papers, Archives of American Art, Smithsonian Institution; photographer unidentified.)

But then one day, Arnold had had enough of ranch life. He found a job with the railroad and tried to convince Solon to go to work with him there. But Solon chose to stay on the California ranch. He would not quit his cowboy dream—not even when his best friend and half-brother Arnold moved back in with the family.

Although Solon missed Arnold and the rest of the family, he was perfectly content being a cowboy on that ranch for a year or two.

Brotherly Bonding

Solon's older brother John Gutzon had always been very independent, as well. Like Solon, Gutzon, lived away from the rest of the family in California. He also enjoyed drawing and painting pictures of horses and old West things. And by then, Gutzon had decided to make art his life's work, so he went to art school in Los Angeles.

Gutzon did not have many friends or much money then, and he may have been very lonely without his brothers, especially Solon. He may have felt much closer to Solon than to the rest of the family. After all, he and Solon were full brothers, and they had many things in common. They had once been the two secret brothers in the family. And they both had a talent for art and a love of horses and the Old West.

They had another bond, too. Solon was earning money on the ranch at that time—and he may have been sending money to his older brother Gutzon, to help him pay for his schooling.[58] In return, Gutzon may have taught Solon some of the things he was learning in art school.

In many ways, that must have been a good time for both brothers, but that big brother/little brother, teacher/student relationship, as John Gutzon sometimes referred to it, would also lead to future problems between those two once-secret brothers, as well.

Chapter 12:
Further Separation

After a year or two in California, Dr. James Borglum and his wife Ida tired of life in busy Los Angeles. They decided to take their children and move back to Omaha.

That did not make Solon happy. He did not want to leave Gutzon. And he did not want to leave his own cowboy life on the California ranch, but he had no choice. His father may have sold his California ranch, or he may have traded his part in it for the chance to use a large area of unbroken ranch land in Central Nebraska near the one-square-mile ranch land he owned there.[59]

Gutzon Stays in California

Everyone in the Borglum family was going back home to Omaha—even Miller and Solon. Everyone, but

Gutzon. By then, Gutzon was caught up in the California art world. He was taking art classes, making friends, and making a name for himself as Gutzon Borglum.

Later, when Gutzon was about twenty, he even married his art teacher Elizabeth "Lisa" Putnam. She was almost twenty years older than he was. She was an artist and an art teacher with connections to many people in America and Europe. She helped Gutzon gain fame.

Gutzon's Fremont Connections

Lisa Borglum had many important friends. One of those was Jessie Fremont, the daughter of Thomas Hart Benton, a Missouri senator (but not the famous artist with the same name). Jessie Fremont was also the widow of the explorer John C. Fremont. (The towns of Fremont in both Nebraska and California were named for him.)

Jessie Fremont introduced Gutzon to many important people in California, New York, and Europe. Gutzon and Lisa even moved to some of those places so he could continue to study art and meet and work with famous artists and other well-known people.

Gutzon and Solon's Art Connections

Gutzon was busy. Although he had little time for

his Omaha family, he would not forget his little brother Solon. Over the years that followed, Gutzon and Solon would continue to learn from each other, inspire each other, and compete with each other. The two of them were sometimes friends and sometimes rivals. They would always make their own way in the world, and the two once-secret-brothers would always be a bit different than their half-brothers.

Solon Feels Lost

Even though Solon had a good relationship with his half-brothers, he often missed his older brother Gutzon and their art connection, especially after Solon returned to Nebraska. Without Gutzon and without the California ranch, Solon felt lost. He did not really know what he wanted to do with his life. But at 17, he felt he was old enough to start making his own way in the world.

Solon was then living in the Borglum family house in Omaha, at 2415 Caldwell Street, near Creighton College. Solon was even listed in the Omaha city directory as a painter. But that art profession was only part of what he wanted to do with his life, and Omaha was not exactly where he wanted to be at that time.

Omaha was becoming a big city—not a frontier town—and Dr. James Borglum was also not sure his son Solon belonged in the city. Solon loved the Old West and working with horses. He was a quiet, adventuresome young man who liked being alone. He missed his old life as a cowboy and seemed unhappy in town.

What To Do with a Ranch

More and more, Solon found himself thinking about that unused Nebraska ranch land his father owned. That seemed like an expensive waste of land to him. But that land was more than 150 miles from the city of Omaha where the family lived. So how could the family run a ranch from that far away?

At that same time, Dr. Borglum was also trying to decide what to do with that central Nebraska ranch land. He and Ida did not want to live on a ranch out in the country. Neither did anyone else in the family—no one but Solon.

Solon remembered how he had loved working with horses and traveling the countryside with his doctor father. He remembered how much he loved spending the night in a bunkhouse or a Plains Indian tipi, or even just sleeping in a bedroll on the prairie. Or working on his California ranch.

Solon dearly missed those Fremont days and the days on his father's California ranch. He really wanted to move to the new ranch in central Nebraska. He wanted to try to build it into a real working cattle ranch.

He told his father that every cowboy wanted to own his own ranch someday. Solon felt he had proven his skills as a real cowboy in California. He said he wanted to try to run his father's new ranch in Nebraska.

As Dr. Borglum listened, he realized that a cattle ranch in the middle of Nebraska just might be a good place for Solon. After all, the Borglums already owned that land. Why not let Solon try to do something with it?

Solon was young and had never run a ranch before, but he was a hardy young man. He was an experienced and resourceful cowhand. He also seemed to be the best son to send to central Nebraska to try to run that ranch.

James Borglum made the decision. Solon would go live on the ranch and do what he could with it.

Solon Borglum, Rancher

Before long, Solon found himself happily heading

west to the near-center of Nebraska—to his father's piece of raw land that was then just a ranch in name only.

Solon may have taken the train to Grand Island station, or he may have traveled all that way by horseback or wagon. From there he traveled fifteen or more miles northwest of Grand Island to where the new town of Cairo (CARE-oh) would soon be built, and then went on four miles further west.

People who already owned land in that area said that they recalled seeing Solon for the first time in or around 1885 or 1886—as a young man of 17 or 18. They first saw him alone, driving a creaky old horse-drawn wagon with a tired old milk cow tied along behind. Solon told the people he met that he was heading for his father's new Loup River Ranch, near Sweet Creek.[60]

That ranch would be very different from the Borglum ranch in California. At that time, there were no buildings on that Nebraska ranch, no fences, no windmills, no cows, no cowboys, no trees—no nothing. Nothing—but the land. A lot of hard work still needed to be done to make it a ranch.

Chapter 13:
An Oasis on the Great American Desert

The Borglums' new Nebraska ranch land was in an area that John C. Fremont and other early American explorers had once called the Great American Desert. That land was raw and rugged. But by the time Solon came to the ranch and the Cairo area in 1885, the surrounding prairie and plains were already changing.

At that time, the Lincoln Land Company was buying up land for the new Grand Island and Wyoming Central Railroad.[61] That new railroad would run north of the Borglum ranch, near the Loup River and its sandhills bluffs. A workforce of gandy dancers (track builders) soon began putting down railroad tracks nearby.

Big House on the Prairie

When the Lincoln Land Company men first came

to that area, they saw a surprise—a showplace house owned by a farmer named George Bussell. His farmhouse was right in the middle of some land that the new railroad company wanted to buy to build a town.

Farmer Bussell liked his place, and he had no intention of selling his land to the railroad. So when the railroad men came to make a deal, he told them he would only sell his farm for an outrageously high price.[62]

Bussell then quoted such a high price for his land that he felt no one could possibly afford it— $20 an acre. In those days, that was extremely high, but of course, the railroad could afford it…and did. The deal was made. The Bussells then moved to a new homestead in southwest Nebraska.

Bussell's two-story house was left right where it was, in the middle of what would become the new town. George Bussell's brother Henry also lived nearby and sold his land to the railroad too. Other building lots were then mapped out around the houses to form a town.

The Town of Cairo

According to local legend, when a land agent or a railroad surveyor first saw the sandy soil there, he said something like, "This place looks like a desert. Let's call this town Cairo." Cairo (KI-ro) was the capital city of Egypt. It was sometimes called "the oasis of the desert."

Cairo then became the name of that railroad town in what people had once called "The Great American Desert" of Nebraska, four miles east of the Borglum ranch. That new town even had streets with such desert sounding names as Egypt, Alexandria, Mecca, and Nile.

But before long, that Nebraska town name of Cairo was no longer pronounced "KI-ro" as in Egypt. Instead, it was pronounced "CARE-oh" just like it looked, or like Karo, the sugary-sweet corn syrup many people put on their pancakes in those days.

Down the Tracks

Cairo was about seven or eight miles from the last small town along that railroad line. Seven to ten miles was a common distance between railroad towns then. That was just far enough to keep the trains running.[63]

Steam powered those trains. That meant water and firewood or coal had to be available at stopover places on the line. So small towns and shipping points grew up every 7 to 10 miles apart along the tracks.[64] (Later, when locomotives were able to travel faster and farther, many of the smaller towns in between died out.)

Another town was built a few miles west of Cairo, along the sandhill bluffs. It was called St. Michael, after Michael Kyne, the first resident there. He gave land to the railroad so that the town would bear his name. Some of Kyne's land just touched the Borglum ranch.

The first train to come through that area along the bluffs was Train #120 in June of 1886. Many ranchers used that railroad to ship their cattle, hogs, and sheep to market. (But in the 1940s, the railroad no longer stopped at St. Michael, and the town died out.)[65]

However, the town of Cairo would survive—a town with a desert-related name, located at the edge of the Nebraska sandhills. In the mid-1880s and the 1890s, Cairo was growing. So were other towns and ranches down the tracks, including the nearly 10,000 acre Taylor Ranch at Ovina, between Cairo and Grand Island.

Ovina is Latin for "sheep," which is what Robert Taylor primarily raised on his nearly 72,000 acres he owned in Nebraska and Wyoming.[66] Like Solon and others in the area, Taylor also raised cattle and horses.

640 Acres or 6,000 Acres?

Early newspaper and magazine articles (and some family members) said the Borglum Ranch near Cairo was approximately 6,000 acres.[67] If so, it would have been more than nine square miles in size. But county land records say the ranch was only 640 acres or one square mile of land. Which is right?

Most likely, Solon used his mile-square 640 acres as his home ranch. But from time to time and in different situations, he may have grazed his cattle on many of the neighboring lands. He may have used open range lands. He may also have leased the extensive pastures, canyons, bluffs, and rivers of some of his neighbors, such as Michael Kyne's bluffs, just west of the Borglum Ranch.

Solon's father had worked for the Union Pacific (U.P.) Railroad before moving to Omaha and had bought his Cairo land from that Omaha-based railroad. So James may have been able to use some land near the tracks to graze his cattle. Or he may have leased grazing rights to some other land areas near the Borglum Ranch.

If so, Solon may have been able to graze his cattle on much more than just his family's 640 acres of land.

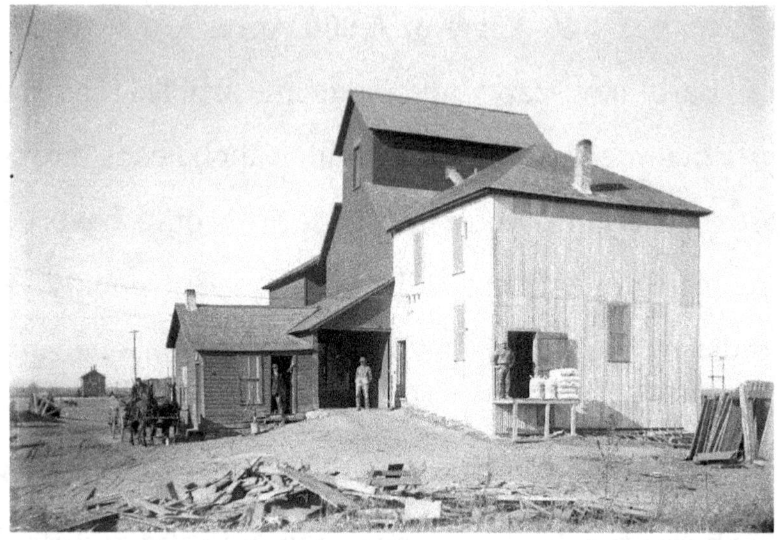

Above: The grain elevator along the railroad tracks at the then-new town of Cairo, Nebraska. See the wagon waiting at the door on the left. Far away in the background to the left is the railroad depot. (Photo courtesy of the Cairo Roots Museum.)

Below: The Cairo Mercantile or general store was one of the first buildings built in the new town of Cairo. This picture was taken a few years later. (Photo courtesy of the Cairo Roots Museum.)

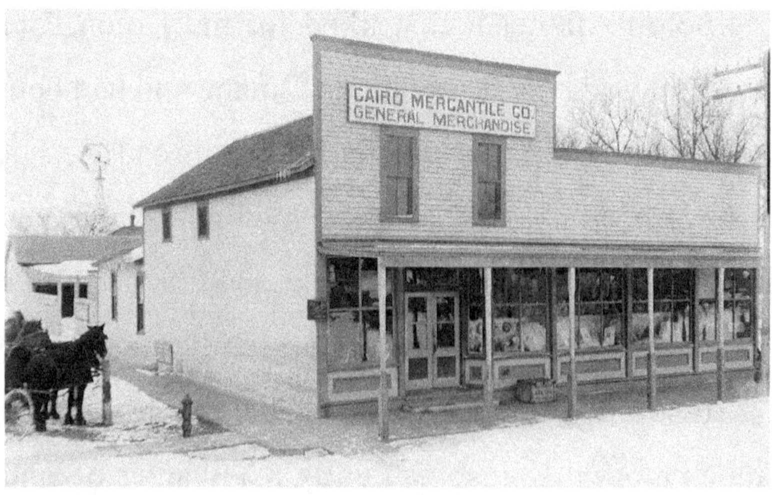

Chapter 14:
At Home on the Range

When Solon Borglum first came to the Cairo area in the mid-1880s, he let the townspeople know he was there to start a ranch on his father's land, about four miles northwest of Cairo. He said he was looking for a good ranch foreman and some cowboys or ranch hands.

He was lucky. He found a good foreman right away. That man's name was Joe Andrews. Joe was an older man and a dependable and experienced cowman. He became a good friend and advisor to Solon. The two men respected each other and worked well together, as if the ranch belonged to both of them.

Right away, the two bosses set off to build the Borglum Ranch. They built a sod house and a dugout. They dug a well for fresh water, "planted corn, cut wild grass for hay, built the bunkhouse," bought a few head of cattle and horses, and planted hundreds of cottonwood trees for windbreaks.[68]

Solon loved living on his ranch near Cairo, on the edge of the Nebraska Sandhills. He lived on the ranch in either a sod house or a dugout—a cave carved into a hillside—or both. Across the road to the east lived his closest neighbors Mr. and Mrs. J. R. Birge.

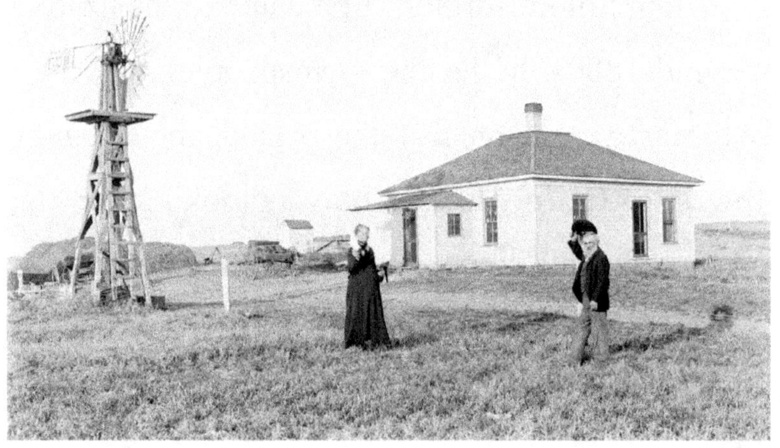

The home of Mr. and Mrs. J.R. Birge, who lived four miles west of Cairo, Nebraska, and just across the road to the east of Solon Borglum's ranch house. (Photo courtesy, Cairo Roots Museum.)

The Boss and His Boys

Solon and Joe also hired other men to help them work the Borglum ranch—"frontiersmen, desperadoes, and hard-drinking cowhands," as Solon's family later called some of them.[69] But they were probably just typical cowboys and even some neighbor boys and young men. Being a cowboy was a rough, tough, dangerous life.

Solon was younger than most of his cowhands and not rough like some of them. He did not drink or swear, and he seldom used a gun, but he was tough enough. Hard work, long hours in the saddle, bad weather, and nights on the cold hard ground did not bother him. He loved that life and worked as hard as the men he called his "boys."

His cowboys respected him and called him "Boss," but he did not boss them around. Every morning, he told them what needed to be done. He had his work to do, and they had theirs.

Then he gave them the freedom to do their jobs as they had time—just as long as those jobs got done. But if he decided a cowhand of his was doing bad things or was "not pulling his weight," then that man was fired and off the property immediately. Everyone liked Solon, but no one argued with him, and no one pushed him around.[70]

A Man of Good Character

Solon was soon well known to the people of the area as a trustworthy and dependable young man. He was so well liked that the people later made him sheriff, but he still seldom, if ever, carried a gun. He could usually do his work without one. People liked and respected him, and he had very few problems keeping the peace.[71]

A Love of Nature

Solon loved working on the ranch with all his "boys"—his ranch hands or cowboys, and his horses and cattle. But he also enjoyed his time alone. In his spare time and in bad weather, he often went outside to enjoy nature and to feel its power. He also did sketches or paintings of things on the ranch—such as his dugout in snow, the ranch animals, and more.

A Need to Learn

There were times when Solon was very busy, and times when work was slow. During slow times, he sometimes felt a need for company and for more learning. At one of those times, he rode his horse a few miles south to a dugout called White Cloud Schoolhouse.

There, Solon enrolled as a student for a few years. He was a bit older than most of the other students, but not too old to learn. He may even have attended school there in 1887 with his youngest half-brother Frank. Frank had been ill and had been sent to the ranch to get well.

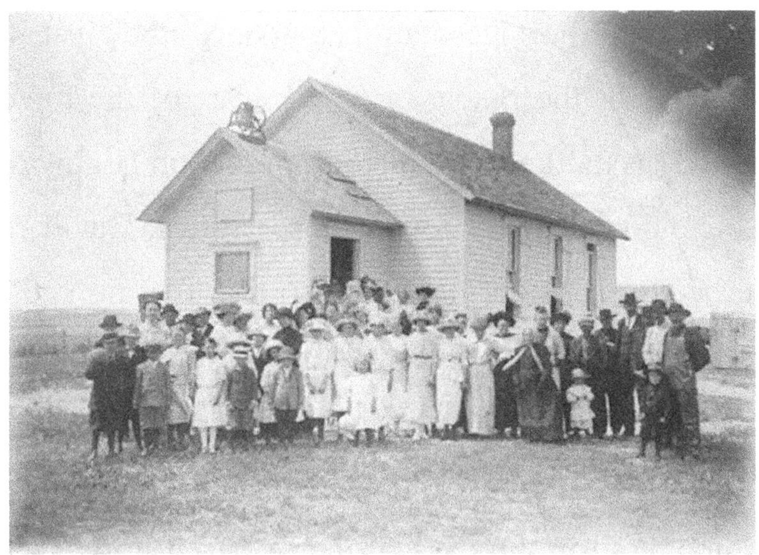

The second White Cloud Schoolhouse, no longer a dugout. Solon helped build this one in the late 1880s or early 1890s, a few miles south of the Borglum Ranch. (Photo credit, Cairo Roots Museum.)

Perhaps Solon went back to school to learn things he had not cared to learn before, or to learn about the history of his new area. He was interested in all that. And there was so much more history there he would have loved to know, if he had only known it existed.[72]

A Love of History

Solon especially loved hearing stories about the Old West from the old-timers, particularly stories about the Plains Indians that he idolized. He may also have heard stories about the early cowboys and settlers, the cavalry, and maybe even the small army camp called Fort

Banishment or Fort Desolation, that once stood just a few miles west of the ranch, or a mile east of the town of Ravenna (as marked by a history marker on Highway 2).

Solon no doubt loved those stories. But it must have been a constant heartache to him that he had just missed living that Old West history by a few decades.

A Review of Those Decades

In the 1860s, Solon's father had walked the Mormon Trail in the days of the overland trails and the Plains Indian Wars. The Pawnee and Lakota were deadly enemies to each other. The Pony Express started and ended. Stagecoaches, telegraphs, and railroads ran west.

By the mid-1870s, the Pawnee had sold off the last of their Nebraska lands and moved to a new reservation in Oklahoma. Homesteads, towns, and ranches started up across the plains. The Plains Indian wars moved to the far northern Plains and the desert southwest. That was ten years before Solon came to his Nebraska ranch.

By the 1880s, ranchers and townspeople settled parts of the Central Plains. More railroads came through. The Lakota and others were reservation people. That was about the time that Solon started his Cairo ranch.

Chapter 15:
The Great Die-Ups

Together, Solon and his foreman Joe kept their cowboys in line and kept that Nebraska ranch working—but it never made any money. That was not their fault. Times were not good, and conditions were against them.

In those days, cattle sometimes still ran free on unfenced miles of "open range," and that first full summer and fall of 1886 was unusually hot and dry. What little grass was able to grow there then was quickly eaten by cattle that had to range far and wide, just to stay alive.

The winter of 1886-1887 followed. It was so bad throughout the northern Great Plains that it was called "The Great Die-Up."[73] Heavy snows fell first, then sudden hot temperatures brought a quick thaw that refroze thickly over what little grass remained. Snow and ice covered that. Cattle that could not get to grass or water died by the thousands in Montana, Wyoming, and the Dakotas. And Nebraska fared only a little bit better.

A Personal Story

Blizzards and bad weather were common on the plains, and sometimes conditions could change in just a matter of minutes. Solon lost a good friend in one such winter storm that started out unusually warm.

One nice warm day, Solon sent his cowboys out to round up what Borglum cattle they could find and bring them back to the ranch. Then Solon went to visit a friend of his on a neighboring ranch. That friend and neighbor was an old man, a "dude" or "a tenderfoot" from the East, who had come west to retire and live out his dream as a cowboy-rancher. He and Solon got along well.

That tenderfoot was just saddling his own horse to go out and bring in his own cattle when Solon stopped to see him that day. Solon offered to have his cowboys round up his friend's cattle. The tenderfoot thanked him but said no. He said he was enjoying himself and looking forward to the ride and to rounding up his cattle himself.

So Solon started back to his own ranch. But before he could get there, the sky turned gray-white. The wind and snow hit hard, causing a whiteout. Solon could barely see anything and only made it home safely because his horse knew the way, and because he knew how to stay out of the low spots that quickly filled with snow.

The snow piled up fast in thick drifts that swirled with the wind, and the whiteness was blinding. By the time, Solon and his own cowboys got his cattle back to the Borglum Ranch headquarters, it was a true blizzard.

The Last Roundup

Later that day, when his cowboys were in the bunkhouse talking, Solon heard something that made him feel sick. Some of his boys had ridden ahead to bring in the cattle herd, but two of the men had turned back to pick up some loose horses that had run off into a canyon. When those cowboys finally found the strays, they saw the two loose horses standing in a low area. There they were being covered by falling and blowing snow.

The cowboys knew the ways of the west. They knew they could not get to those horses and could not help them. The horses would have to try to survive the storm on their own. If the cowboys stayed out any longer, they and their horses could die, too.

By that time, Solon's cowboys could hardly see to get back to the ranch buildings. Along the way, they noticed a saddled horse trying to push its way through a deep snowdrift. But they could not get to the struggling horse through the swirling snow and deep drifts. They were lucky to find their own way back to the ranch.

While those cowboys told about seeing that saddled horse, other men in the bunkhouse wondered aloud about the identity of the missing rider. At that moment, a chill probably ran up and down Solon's spine. He knew immediately that his tenderfoot friend was out there, somewhere, probably on the ground where he had fallen or where he had been thrown from his saddled horse. But there was no way to help or to find the tenderfoot during such a storm. And afterwards, it would be too late. Solon knew his friend had already gone on his last roundup.[74]

Remembering the Story

Solon would long remember that night. In his mind, he pictured that empty-saddled horse pushing through the deep swirling snow, trying to stay alive, trying to make it home. Years later, Solon made a small snow-white sculpture of a saddled horse, calling it *The Last Roundup,* in memory of his lost friend and that empty-saddled horse.

To most people that little white sculpture is nothing much. The features of the horse are not even clearly defined, as if snow and wind still whip across the lone figure. But to anyone who knows its history, that small *Last Roundup* sculpture is a story in itself—the story of a struggling horse and a missing rider—the story of a friend who lost his horse and his life in a blizzard.

Solon would draw many pictures of his ranch, some with deep drifts of snow covering the buildings. He would store up other memories and stories in his head. He would turn many of those memories into artworks—drawings, paintings, and sculptures—each one telling a story, if people just knew how to look at and read them.[75]

The School Children's Blizzard

Nebraska, Minnesota, and Iowa had some even worse weather the following winter of 1887-1888. In Nebraska, that winter was known as the year of "The School Children's Blizzard," because so many country-school children and their teachers were caught in the snow on their way home, especially on one afternoon.

There had already been one snowstorm in early January that year. Then about a week later, on January 12, 1888, the weather turned unusually warm…at first. But before long, the temperature suddenly dropped. In some places, it fell 60 to 100 degrees in just over 24 hours of time, as an unexpected blizzard hit.[76] The snow, wind, and cold came on so suddenly that people had almost no time to get to safety.

As many as 235 people may have died that day across the Great Plains. Many of them were children.[77] One of the heroes of that terrible day was Minnie Freeman, a teenaged teacher near Ord, Nebraska, who led her students to safety after the wind tore the door and the roof off their country schoolhouse. Ord was only about 55 miles north of the Borglum Ranch.

The End of The Open Range

The blizzards of the mid-1880s made ranchers realize they needed to keep their herds closer to home. To do that they needed fences, especially a new kind of fence called barbed wire. They also needed windmills to make groundwater available for ranch animals, and they needed hayfields to provide feed for their animals during bad times. Those new things were good for ranchers, but they also forced cowboys to spend more time doing farm work—fixing fences and windmills, and putting up and feeding hay—and less time cowboying.

The Old West was dying, and Solon greatly missed those old days and ways. He even wrote a magazine article about the dying off of cowboys, sheriffs, and other "good men" of the West.[78]

But Solon was fortunate: He had his own memories of cowboying, and he would use them to create his own artworks to remind himself of the old days.

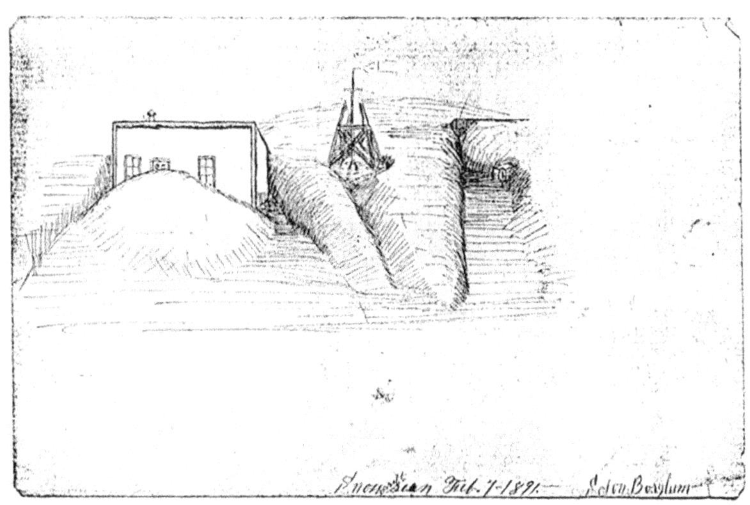

Solon's 1891 sketch of a snowstorm on his home place at his Nebraska ranch, showing snow on a haystack in front of the bunkhouse and dug-out paths between the windmill, bunkhouse, and pens. (Photo credit: Cairo Roots Museum.)

Chapter 16:
Carved in Sand

Solon loved the look and feel of the land, its nature, and its weather. He even found beauty in the violent power of blizzards, thunderstorms, and tornadoes.[79] He was at home outdoors. And as a cowboy, it was natural for him to work outside, even in storms, to feed and protect his animals. That was his life then, and all those elements would show up in his art.

Sometimes, he drew what he saw and knew—horses, cattle, cowboys. At other times he walked the land, looking for pits of natural clay that he used to make small sculptures of those things and those times.[80]

Cowboy At Rest

Sometimes, Solon even rode his horse up one of the nearby tall bluffs, to where he could look out over the land all around him. There, he would dismount and lie down on the top of a sandhill to watch the wind ruffle the grasses of the prairie below him, and to see what he could see, while his horse stood or grazed next to him.

When people saw him doing that, they sometimes thought he was lazy.[81] They did not understand that he was working on a different job. He was studying things and storing up memories for his artist life later on.

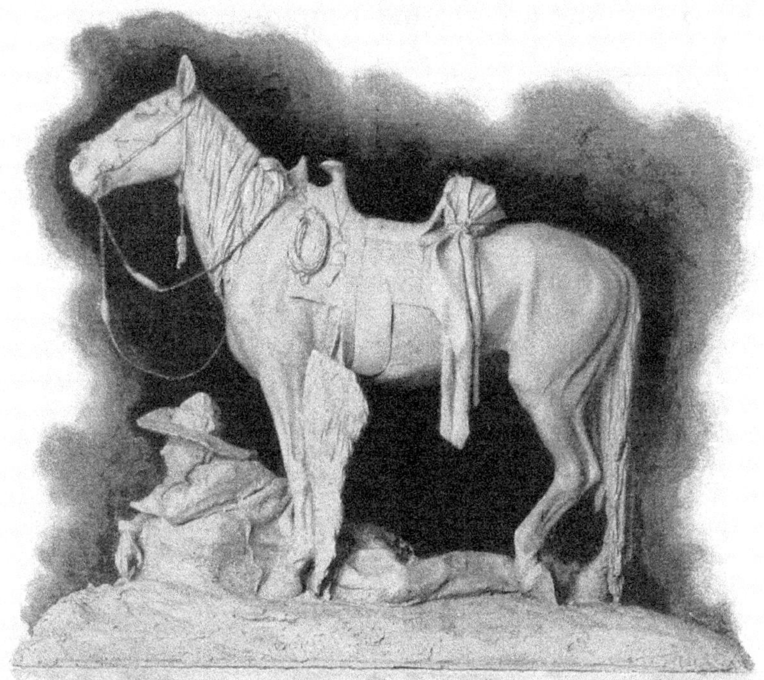

Cowboy At Rest by Solon Borglum was sculpted many years later and may have been a self-portrait of his earlier days when he rode his horse to the top of a sandhills bluff near Cairo, Nebraska. There, he watched the wind move in waves across the grasses in the valleys below. (Photo of that sculpture in clay by Solon Borglum from a 1904 issue of *The Century* magazine.)

Indian in the Sandhill

Solon also loved the history and legends of his Nebraska land, and he loved the Plains Indians who had once lived not far away. One day while wandering the bluffs he may have been thinking about those Plains Indian people who once hunted in that same area.

He may even have heard about a Chief White Cloud. Legend said that the chief and his warriors had once stolen some gold from a train many miles away. But the chief was wounded. Legend says he hid the gold in the bluffs at St. Michael. Then he died. His warriors buried him there, near the top of a sandhill bluff.[82]

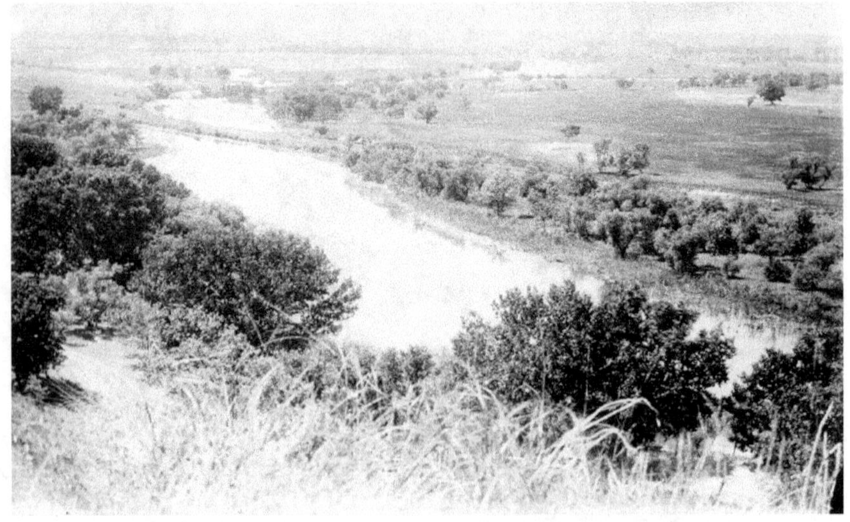

A view Solon may have seen often in the 1880s from the top of the bluffs near his ranch and St. Michael, Nebraska, looking north. (Photo courtesy, Cairo Roots Museum.)

One day, Solon had an idea to use those bluffs as a canvas for a special art project, a tribute to Native Americans, maybe even to honor White Cloud who may have stolen the gold to help his people. Solon wanted to picture and honor those Plains Indians that he admired.

So Solon carved a huge Native American face and figure into the side of one of the sandhills bluffs, possibly Kyne's Bluff itself. It must have been difficult, and it probably took a while to carve something that big in the sandy soil of such a tall hill.

Not many people lived there, but many nearby people used that area for recreation purposes. Some of those hills may even have been on part of the land Solon used for his cattle. No one seemed to mind that he used those hills for his art project, too.

There was no Highway 2 there then, so few people noticed the huge figure of at least one Plains Indian—hand-carved into the side of that bluff by Solon Borglum. But at least a few people did. Old-timers said the big carving was still recognizable as a Plains Indian in 1906, about 20 years after it was carved. That was near the time Indian bones were found buried in the bluff.[83]

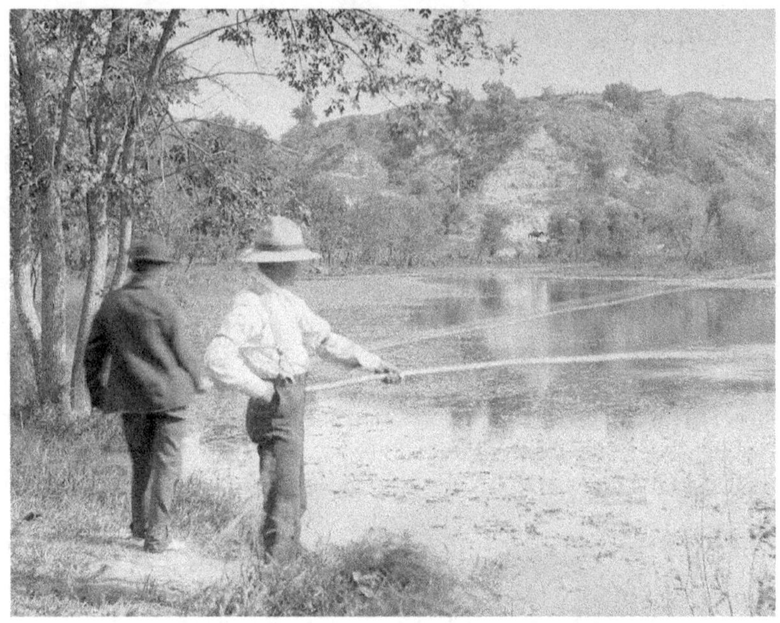

Above: Unidentified men fishing at a lake at the St. Michael bluffs, late 1800s. (Photo by Henry S. Balcom of Cairo, photo courtesy of the Cairo Roots Museum.)

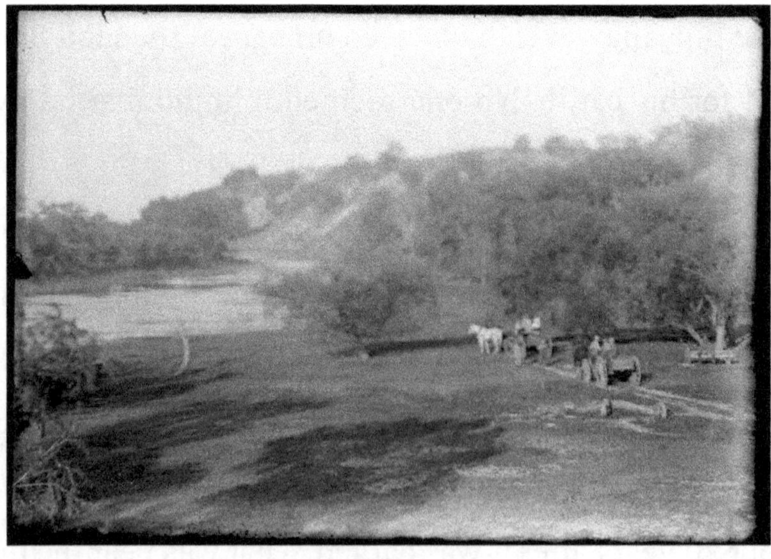

Above: Another photo of the river and the bluffs at St. Michael, Nebraska. (Photo courtesy of the Cairo Roots Museum.)

Bones in the Bluff

Some people in the area believed the legend about Chief White Cloud. Many even searched the bluffs for gold for years, but no one ever found it. Some said it was just a story. But Solon would have loved that story—and would have loved living there when it happened.

In a way he had. Years later, in 1907, a local newspaper and the *Nebraska State Historical Society Magazine* reported the finding of Native American bones, possibly those of a chief, in an early 1870s grave on top of one of the highest of those hills. That may have been Kyne's Bluff, overlooking Sweet Creek, near the Loup River—near the Borglum Ranch.[84] As strange as it may seem, the man who found those bones was a visiting nephew of the Hodgson Brothers. The Hodgsons had sometimes worked for Solon on his ranch.[85]

Solon ranched in that area from 1885 until 1893. That means he moved there about 15 years after the chief's burial and left the area about 15 years before the grave was found. Solon would have loved knowing just how close he may have come to meeting some of those Plains Indian people he had idolized.

Lost Forever

A local woman who moved onto Solon Borglum's home ranch years later—and whose family owned most of the bluffs in those later years—wrote in a newspaper article that the Indian grave was found on the northeast side of the easternmost bluff. She said Solon's Indian carvings were on the southeast side of that same bluff.[86]

People from that area said that the easternmost hill or Kyne's Bluff was honeycombed with deep caves, some up to 100 feet long. That bluff was close to both Sweet Creek and the Loup River, so it was close to the Borglum Ranch. Local people say that Kyne's bluff has since caved in and collapsed during a flood when the rivers changed course, washing away the sandy base.[87]

The Indian bones had already been removed and studied by then. They have probably been reburied with other native bones by now. So nothing remains of Solon's carvings in the sand or of the chief's grave, except the words of the people who once saw them.[88]

Brothers on the Ranch

Other Borglum family members may also have noticed Solon's big Plains Indian carvings. While Solon was running the ranch, some of his half-brothers came to stay there with him, now and then, including half-brothers Arnold, Miller, and youngest brother Frank. Solon even taught Frank how to draw while he was there.

Many people believe that Solon's full brother John Gutzon lived on the ranch. Gutzon did visit there a few times, but he did not live there. By that time, he was living and working as an artist in California and Europe. (But years later, Gutzon did have his own big cattle ranch in South Dakota while carving Mount Rushmore.)

High Praise

One day in 1890, Gutzon and his wife Lisa left California and did stop to visit Solon at the Loup River ranch in Nebraska. Gutzon and Lisa were on their way to Omaha to see the rest of the Borglum family. From there, they were going to New York and then to Europe.

While visiting at the ranch, older brother Gutzon looked at all of Solon's artwork that was pasted up on the ranch house walls.[89] Solon and Gutzon then probably went together to the bluffs to see Solon's monumental-sized carving of the Plains Indian in the sandhill. They may even have done some carving there together.[90]

Gutzon had been studying art from master artists and teachers around the world. He was already creating masterworks of his own. But in those days, most of his art still consisted of drawings and paintings.

Gutzon was impressed by Solon's work, and most impressed by his carvings in the bluffs. (Such artworks probably inspired Gutzon to begin to carve mountains of his own, thirty-some years later.)

While visiting the ranch at that time, Gutzon praised Solon. He told his younger brother that he had real talent and advised him to quit ranching and go east or to Paris to study art. "Solon," Gutzon reportedly said, "you should be an artist!"[91]

A New Way of Thinking

That praise started Solon thinking. The Borglums' Loup River and Sweet Creek Ranch had never made much money, but Solon had always believed that "maybe next year" it just might. He loved the ranch and its way of life. But when Gutzon praised his artwork, Solon began thinking about leaving the ranch and taking up another of his loves and his other chosen occupation—working as an artist.

That possibility interested Solon, and he began to think about it seriously. But he would not leave the ranch completely for three more years—not until his older brother Gutzon came home again from Europe in 1893.

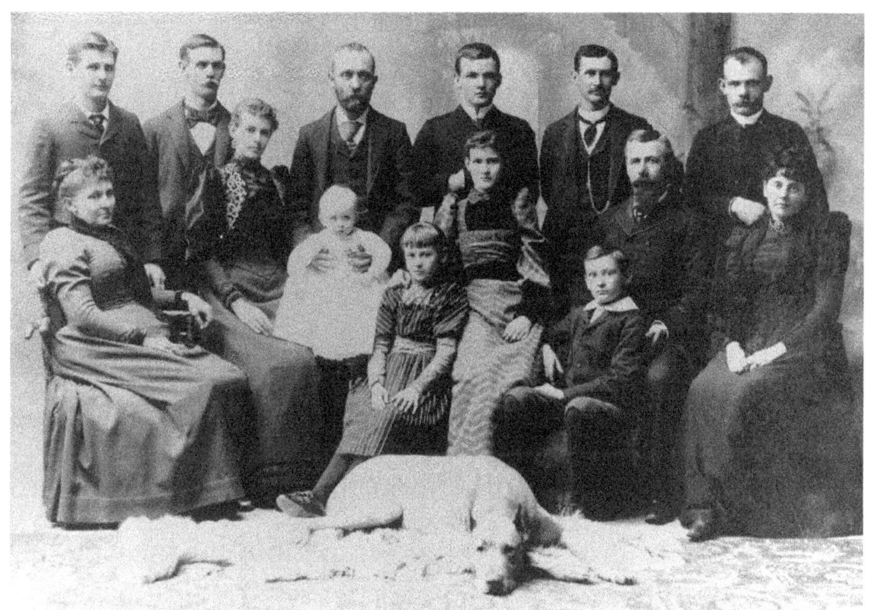

Borglum family portrait, June 1893, left to right, back row, men: Arnold, August, Alfred Darlow (husband of eldest daughter Anna), Solon, Miller, and Gutzon. Front rows: Ida (mother/stepmother), Anna, baby Ida (Anna and Alfred's baby; first grandchild), Harriet, Theodora ("Dora"), Frank/Francis, James (father), Lisa Borglum (Gutzon's first wife), and one of Gutzon's Great Dane dogs. (Unidentified photographer. Photo courtesy of Solon H. Borglum and Borglum family papers, Archives of American Art, Smithsonian Institution.)

Chapter 17:
Leaving His Land

Solon loved living on the ranch, but he hated to see the Old West dying. In December 1890, around the time of his 22nd birthday, he heard about the death of the great Lakota chief Sitting Bull. Soon after that, Solon heard about the killing of many Lakota people by the cavalry just north of the Nebraska-South Dakota border at a place called Wounded Knee—just a few hundred miles northwest of his ranch.

Solon loved Native American people and felt very sad about their terrible loss of life and culture. He knew it was another end to the Old West and the freedom of the Plains Indians. He seemed to feel that loss personally.

Thinking about Art

At the same time, Solon could not stop thinking

about what his brother Gutzon had told him. Solon wondered if he really had art talent. Or was Gutzon just saying what Solon wanted to hear?

There was one way to find out. Solon decided to take some time off now and then and go to Omaha to take art classes from well-known artist J. Laurie Wallace over the next three years. He loved doing that, but in between those classes, he always came back home to the ranch.

Each time Solon returned to the ranch, he found himself spending more and more time working on his art and less time doing ranchwork. Then in 1893, he heard that Gutzon and Lisa were coming back from Paris with three Great Dane dogs they had bought in Europe. They planned to stop in Omaha to see the Borglum family before taking the train back to California again.

One-Man Show

Solon was really excited about seeing his older full-brother. He collected all his own artworks from his ranch and took them back to their father's house in Omaha. There, he put them on display in the basement, along with all the artworks he had done in his Omaha art classes.

At the family house, Solon showed his brother Gutzon all his artworks, even the smallest pieces, drawn on the back of tiny scraps of wrapping paper. Gutzon praised Solon's work and invited him to come to California to live with him and Lisa. He said Solon could use his studio and could take art lessons there from him and from Lisa.[92]

Solon was so happy with that idea that he decided to sell his part of the ranch. He wanted to leave for California right away. And he made plans to do just that.

There was just one problem. Gutzon had invited his brother Solon to come to California, to live there with him in his home, to share a studio, and to take classes from him and Lisa. But Gutzon had not asked Lisa if that was okay with her. And it definitely was not!

But it was too late to cancel the invitation. Solon was already on his way to California.

Unwanted Guest

Gutzon's house in California was very small—with no room for Solon. But Lisa did loan him a blanket so he could sleep outside with the huge Great Dane dogs. Solon did not mind. He loved camping out and living on the land, and he had his art to keep him busy.

At first, Lisa and Gutzon tried to teach Solon how to draw and paint in the old European and romantic styles of art. That was the way Gutzon had been taught by Lisa, and that was the way they wanted Solon to paint. But the two brothers had very different ways of creating art.

Solon had his own natural style of drawing, painting, and sculpting. It was a style he liked and one that worked well with the way he had been taught in Omaha. He did not want to change his ways.

Solon's art style was also a somewhat harsh but realistic approach to western American art. That style was rapidly gaining fame and popularity in America and Europe, especially in France. In France, such art was sometimes called Beaux Arts (pronounced Boze Arts).

Solon was good at that kind of art, and he refused to change his style, even for his brother. Solon was also more interested in sculpting than in drawing and painting, but his brother Gutzon was not yet ready to do much sculpting. So Solon worked and waited, hoping for a time when he and his brother might sculpt together. Sadly, that did not happen.

By that time, Solon was generally taking care of things at Gutzon and Lisa's studio—and taking care of the dogs. But soon Solon began to feel more like an unpaid worker than an artist. He did not mind working or cleaning up the studio, but he did not like the way Lisa bossed him around, tried to change him, and treated him like one of the dogs.[93]

Of course, things were not easy for Lisa, either. She had to share her husband, her small home, and her studio, with her brother-in-law and the dogs. She was an artist and teacher, but her student-husband was becoming more famous than she was. And her brother-in-law Solon was just as talented but less willing to listen to her.

She must have felt left out and angry, so she made life difficult for Solon. She even seemed to do everything she could to try to force him to leave.[94]

On His Own

One day Solon did leave. He just went for his usual morning hike through the Sierra Madre Mountains, taking only what he could carry with him—but this time, he also took his clothes, his art supplies, the blanket, and a small campstove that he often used. He just walked away and never came back. He did not even say good-bye. He was a grown man, and a very independent and adventurous one.

Gutzon Leaves Too

Not long after Solon left Gutzon's home and studio in late 1894 or early 1895, Gutzon became restless, too. He missed Solon. He became so lonely and restless without his brother that he decided to take Lisa and go back to Europe. This time they settled in England. Not long after that, Gutzon's slightly younger half-brother August joined them in England and began studying music there.

Chapter 18:
Drawn to Horses

After leaving Gutzon's house, Solon happily hiked across California alone, enjoying the outdoors and nature, sleeping out, eating almost nothing but cooked oatmeal and crackers. And like a magnet to steel, wherever he wandered, he was always drawn to ranches or stables and horses. Horses were always one of his greatest loves, and they would always be a part of his life.

Occasionally, he took jobs drawing and painting pictures of people and racehorses. He was happy doing that, but he missed his Nebraska sandhills and sculpting.

Solon made many friends in California. One of those was a science professor who hired him to make illustrations for his science lectures. Soon other people came to Solon to have portraits or other artworks done.

Back to School

Solon's new friends kept encouraging him to sell his artworks and to take the money and go east to the Cincinnati Art Institute. One day he decided to do just that, with letters of recommendation from his professor friend. He had some money from his art sales and some other money sent to him by his half-brother Arnold.

Solon arrived at the Cincinnati Art Institute and became a student there in November 1895. He was 27-years-old, older than most of the other students. He was also late. School had already started a month before.

Because he knew no one there, Solon was rather lonesome. He was also homesick for the wild country, and so he often went walking. As usual, he found a stable full of horses.

He would stop at that stable every morning before school, so he could study the horses and draw them.[95] Before long, he began using clay to make a beautiful but sad model of two horses. That small sculpture called *Horse Pawing a Dead Horse* was made in his Beaux Arts style. It was probably based on one of the Plains stories he knew so well from his time on his Nebraska ranch.

When the sculpture was finished, Solon invited Louis Rebisso (Loo-us Ruh-bee-so), one of his art professors, to come see it. The teacher was very impressed with Solon's talent. He entered that sculpture into the school's yearly competition, even though he knew it could not win, because it had been created outside of art class.

Of course, the sculpture was disqualified, but its entry brought attention to Solon's work. The school gave Solon a $50 prize and also a scholarship to pay for his next year of schooling. Then Professor Rebisso invited Solon to live with the Rebisso family and to use an art studio at their home. Solon happily accepted.[96]

Solon finally knew what he wanted to do with his life. He wanted to sculpt the things he loved—to make Old West art, to tell the stories of the horses, cowboys, and Plains Indians he had known.

The next year, Solon created 17 sculptures that were entered in the school's yearly competition. He earned many honors and awards and received another scholarship to the Cincinnati art school for the following year. An agent also sold some of his artworks for him.[97]

To Europe to Look Around

Solon then decided to celebrate by going to Paris to look around for a few months, just as Gutzon had once told him to do. But Solon had very little money, so he traveled across the ocean by working on a cattle boat. He intended to return to Cincinnati by Christmas to start the new school term there, but his plans would change.[98]

On his way to Paris, Solon stopped in London to see his brother Gutzon. They were both becoming famous, and they were worried people would confuse the two of them because they were both artists with strange given names and the same last name of Borglum.

At that time, Gutzon seemed to prefer painting and drawing to sculpting, and Solon seemed to prefer sculpting to drawing and painting.[99] The two brothers hoped that staying within their chosen art forms would be enough to keep people from mis-identifying them, but history proved that would not stop the confusion.

Looking Around in Paris

Solon soon left his full-brother Gutzon and their half-brother August in England and went on to France. Solon had never really liked big cities, so he did not expect to like Paris. And at first, he did NOT!

Paris was big, busy, and very foreign to Solon who did not speak French. He studied the buildings there and toured the museums and art galleries. Sometimes he drew or painted things that caught his attention, but generally it was an unhappy time for him. He had little money for food, or a room, or sculpting, and he had no friends there.

In that land of beauty so far from home, Solon again found himself lonely and longing for the windswept sandhills, the majestic mountains, and the rugged countryside of the West, with its horses, stories, and strange natural beauty. He wanted to go back, but he did not know what to do to get back there.

One day, he took a last walk through Paris. It was a sort of goodbye tour. While walking, he ran into another young artist who introduced him to an American sculptor named Bela Pratt. Pratt was also studying at an art school in Paris. The sculptors quickly became friends.

Pratt had two studios at his place. He offered Solon one of the rooms as a studio apartment. Pratt also introduced him to other American artists in Paris.[100] Before long Solon would become famous in France too.

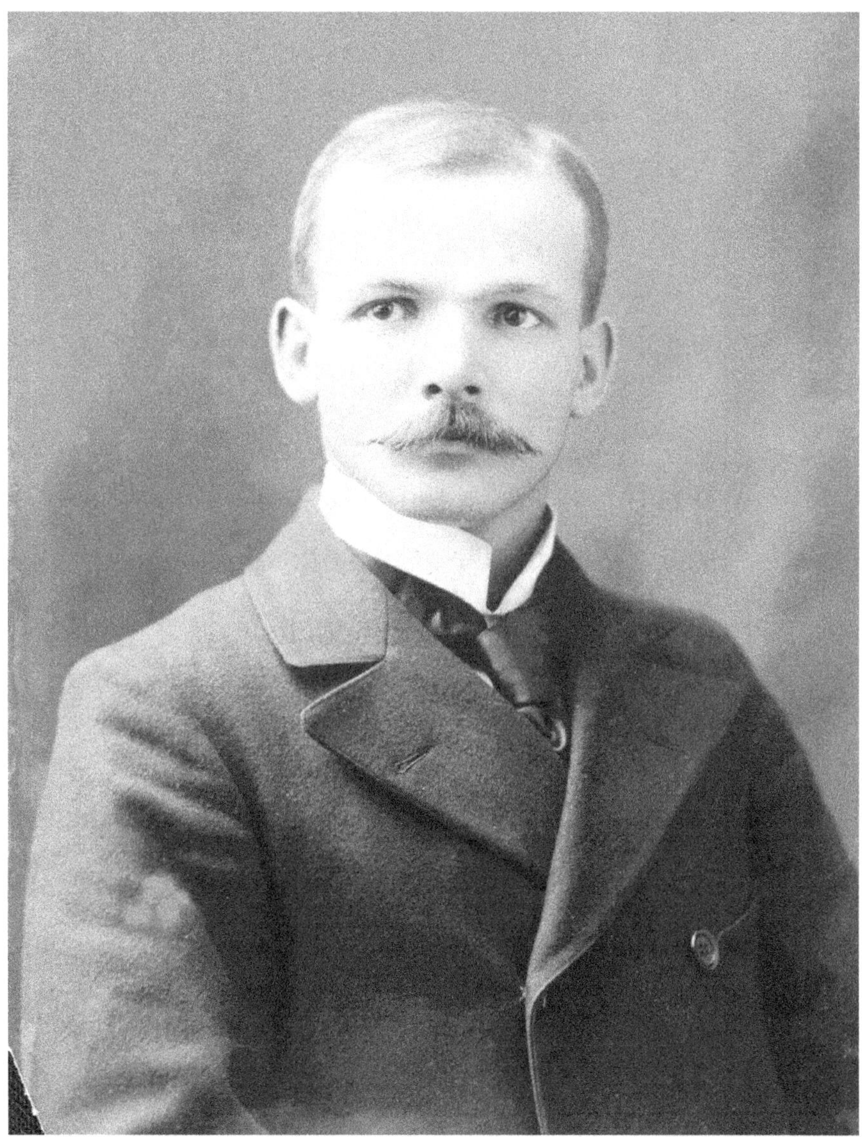

Solon H. Borglum in the late 1890s. (Photo by unidentified photographer, Solon H. Borglum and Borglum family papers, Archives of American Art, Smithsonian Institution.)

Chapter 19:
Inspired By Horses

With friends and a place to stay, Solon began to look at Paris differently. But he still went walking when he was lonesome. One day, he happened again—as he often did—to come across a stable full of horses.

A stable was not unusual in those days, not even in Paris. Cars were not around yet. Horses were still the way to travel. Horses pulled carts, carriages, and cabs. And Solon always seemed to find horses wherever he went. He loved them, and they seemed to enjoy being with him.

At that Paris stable, Solon found happiness again with the horses. He could not speak French, but he could use hand signs, like he had often used with the Plains Indians as a kid. In that way, he told the Frenchmen at the stable that he just wanted to be around horses.

Memories of Mustangs

At the stable, Solon spent time with each of the horses, and he soon noticed something odd. A few of the animals looked very different. They did not look like the tall sleek horses of Paris. They looked like the rough ponies the Plains Indians rode, or like the ones Solon's cowboys rode on his Nebraska ranch. They were indeed horses of wild mustang blood! But mustangs in Paris? How could that be? Mustangs were American horses.

Solon questioned the cabbies. Through sign language and words, the men told him that Buffalo Bill Cody's Wild West Show had just been in Paris. And when it was time for the show to go back to America, Cody had run short on money. So he had sold some of the show's mustangs to the Paris stable owner.[101]

Solon was excited by that discovery. He took it as a sign that he was in the right place at the right time. After all, Cody was a Nebraskan with a ranch at North Platte, about 150 miles west of the Borglum Ranch at Cairo.

Solon also realized that Cody's mustangs were just what he needed to create a special piece of artwork in Paris. But first he needed something else from America.

Saddling Up

Solon sent a message home to his father, asking him to send some western tack from the ranch—western saddles, saddle blankets, bridles, halters, lariats, and more—two of each thing. He knew he needed that cowboy gear to help him create an authentic piece of Old West sculpture in Europe.

With the mustangs, and his new friends, and a new way of looking at things, Solon came to realize just how different his own sculptures were. They were not just different in style, but also in what they portrayed, as well as in the message they sent, and in the stories they told.

European art was often classical, romantic, and sometimes soft and sweet. But as always, Solon found himself wanting to make more of his rough, rugged, and realistic Old West American art, this time in France.

When the saddles and other tack arrived, Solon went right to work. He saddled the mustangs and put a scene together as a model for a sculpture called *Lassoing Wild Horses.* It showed two cowboys on horseback, one riding and swinging a rope, and one whose horse had fallen, while chasing other unseen horses.

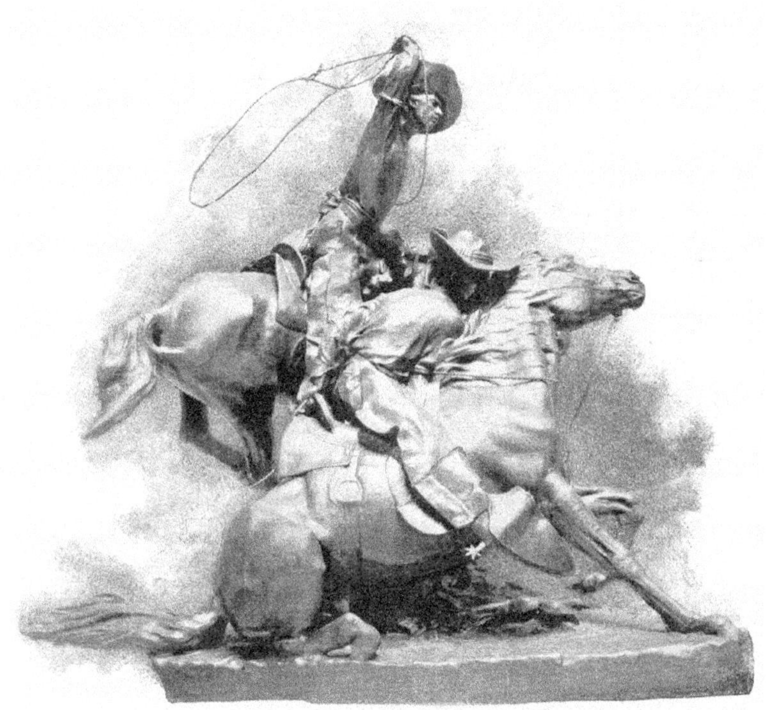

Lassoing Wild Horses by Solon H. Borglum. (From a photo of the sculpture in bronze by Solon H. Borglum as printed in a 1904 issue of *The Century* magazine.)

As that sculpture neared completion, Bela Pratt commented that, as an artist, Solon Borglum was a "born genius." Pratt then invited some of his artist friends in to see what he called "Borglum's Cowboys."[102]

One of those American visitors and artists was Augustus Saint-Gaudens. He and other artists liked Solon's sculpture, but they also offered him bits of valuable advice. This time, Solon was pleased to listen and to learn from those more experienced artist-teachers.

Staying in France

Before long, Solon's sculpture was completed to everyone's satisfaction. Saint-Gaudens then encouraged Solon to stay in Paris and to go to school with him and Pratt. Solon wanted to do that, but he had a paid scholarship waiting for him in Ohio.

Solon contacted his teachers at the Cincinnati art school and told them about his good fortune. They agreed that he should stay in France. They also made arrangements to transfer his 1898 American scholarship to the Beaux Arts College in Paris.

There, Solon showed his new sculpture and others in several major art contests. His works earned him great honors and some money—but he never cared much about money. At the same time, he rented a studio with an artist named Alphaeus (Al-FAY-us) Cole. There Solon began work on another life-size sculpture of wild horses.

By then, Solon was making quite a name for himself at the Beaux Arts College. He was accepted as an award-winning student and a talented artist with many friends in the art world. He was well on his way to becoming famous as a real artist of the Old West, in Paris.

Telling His Stories in Art

As some of his friends often noted, Solon was special. They said that many people went on to art school to develop a talent, but they really had nothing to say. But Solon had done things the other way around: He had lived in the West and worked as a cowboy. He had lived that life and loved it, and he had wonderful stories to tell. Then he studied art and learned how to tell those stories through his artworks.[103] That made his art more real and far more meaningful. Some of the best Western and Old West artists would learn their art craft that same way, including Frederick Remington and Charles Russell, who would often be compared to and with Solon.

Chapter 20:
The Cowboy and His Lady

In those days, Solon was happily creating his Old West art in Europe. His art would not wait, and he had no time for anything else, except his friendship with artists.

But one day, Clement Barnhorn came to Paris. He was the new director of the Cincinnati school of art where Solon had been a student. Barnhorn had come to Paris to visit friends, the Vignal (Veen-YAWL) family.

Jean (Jhawn) Vignal was a French Baptist minister. He and his wife Lydie (LID-ee) were refined people of culture. They had two very musically talented daughters—Emma was a singer, and Lucy played piano.

The Vignal family lived in a lovely house in Paris. They enjoyed the arts and entertaining, and they often gave music recitals at their home. Guests included other musicians, playwrights, and artists, such as Alphaeus Cole (who shared a studio with Solon), and Clement Barnhorn of the Cincinnati art school.

One day, the talk at the Vignal home naturally turned to Alpaheus's studio partner Solon Borglum, who also had ties to Barnhorn's Cincinnati art school. At that time, Solon was the star of the Beaux Arts School in Paris, and Solon's sculpture *Lassoing Wild Horses* was then on display at a big local show.

The Vignal sisters did not know Solon. So Barnhorn made arrangements for them to visit the gallery to see Solon's sculpture. Barnhorn also asked Solon to talk with the girls, but Solon was busy working with other artists at that time. His art took up all his time, energy, and money, and he had no interest in meeting women.

However, all that changed when the two Vignal sisters walked into the gallery. Solon watched them from a distance as they walked around and looked at his artwork. Much to his surprise, he found that he really liked them, especially the sister named Emma.

The next day, Solon asked Barnhorn to introduce him to the sisters. Barnhorn did, and that spring, Emma guided Solon, Barnhorn, and two Cincinnati art teachers all around Paris. The following summer, Solon took care of Emma's dog for her while the Vignal family was away visiting in England. And to his surprise, Solon soon realized that both he and the dog really missed Emma.

By the time the Vignals returned from England, Solon's priorities had changed. He visited Emma at her family home often. Three weeks later, he and Emma were engaged, and on December 10, 1898, they were married. Solon was just 12 days short of 30 years old. Emma was 34. Soon after that, Solon's studio partner and friend Alpaheus Cole painted Emma's portrait. That portrait was then put on permanent display in Solon's studio.[104]

Solon and Emma had no time then for a honeymoon. Solon was finishing his work on another life-size statue called *Stampede of Wild Horses*. That sculpture was then entered in an exhibit at a Paris show where it received Honorable Mention, as "one of the best and most noticeable things in the sculpture gallery."[105]

Chapter 21:
Honeymoon on the Plains

Six months after their wedding, Solon and his wife Emma finally left on their honeymoon, but the bride had no idea what she was getting herself into. The well-educated lady from Paris—with her fine manners and beautiful clothes—was leaving her parents' fine house, her servants, and her rich life in Paris for a trip to America, but not just anywhere in America.

She and her new husband were going to the Crow Creek Indian Reservation on the plains of central South Dakota to stay with the Dakota Sioux people. The Dakota were related to the Lakota Sioux who had hunted in Nebraska. (Crow Creek Reservation was 242 miles east of what would become Mount Rushmore, the monument Solon Borglum's brother Gutzon would later carve.)

Arrangements and Delays

One of Solon's Nebraska ranch buddies had made arrangements with a missionary for the newly-weds to stay on that reservation for four months. Emma's brother Paul Vignal was a French Army officer, stationed at the French embassy in Washington D.C. at that time. Paul had made the financial arrangements for the visit.[106]

Solon even had the perfect date set for the newly-weds' arrival at the reservation—the 4th of July, 1899. For that day only, the Dakota Sioux people had received permission to dress up and do things in their old ways. They could gather together and enjoy their native ways of life, feasting, singing, dancing, and more.[107]

Solon wanted to be there in time to see all that. He also wanted to sketch those Plains Indian people that he so respected and admired—while he could—before their old culture was lost forever.

The honeymoon couple traveled by ship to America, somewhat like Solon's parents had once done. Then they took a train to South Dakota. But the train arrived late in the town of Chamberlain on the 4th of July, so they missed the stage to Fort Thompson. By 6 P.M., they still had 30 miles to go—and there was no stagecoach to take them, and no riding horses either.[108]

Trouble Crossing the Plains

Emma was not a hardy person, but she loved her husband. She was willing to go anywhere with him. In a letter to friends and family, she later wrote that they were having supper in Chamberlain when a scary-looking cowboy named Rattlesnake Jim told them that he could take them to the reservation. The Borglums accepted—but Jim's horses were not in Chamberlain. He had to go get them first.[109]

The couple waited two hours, but Rattlesnake Jim was still not back. Then, another cowboy agreed to take them. They started out that cold dark night, with fireworks going off all around them.

They had no light to guide them. The wagon horses just walked in deep trail ruts that cut across the country. Once, the horses spooked and ran off so suddenly the newly-weds fell off the seat and landed on the floor of the wagon. Later, one of the horses almost drowned after falling in the mud while crossing a river. By then, they feared they might not make it to the reservation alive.[110]

After resting the horses, they started out again, under the threat of rain. Hours later, they reached the reservation, just as the sky started to get light. But they were already one day late! To make matters worse, their hosts had not received their letter and were not expecting them—but the hosts were still very glad to see them.[111]

To their great joy, the newly-weds then found that the Native American celebration on the reservation had been extended one more day. So they were just in time!

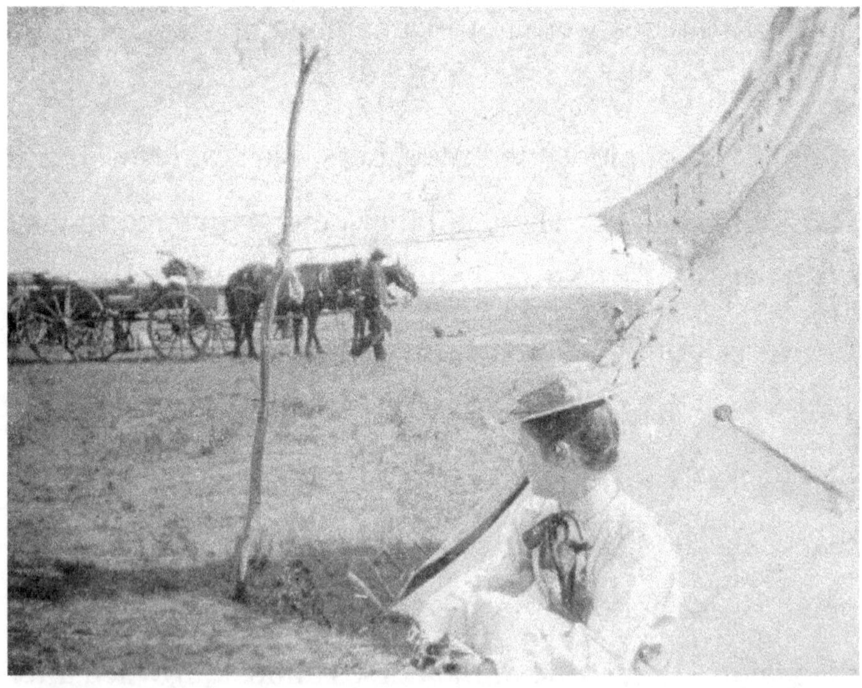

Solon's wife Emma on her honeymoon by a tipi (teepee) at Crow Creek Reservation, 1899. (Photo by unidentified photographer, courtesy of Solon H. Borglum and Borglum family papers, Archives of American Art, Smithsonian Institution.)

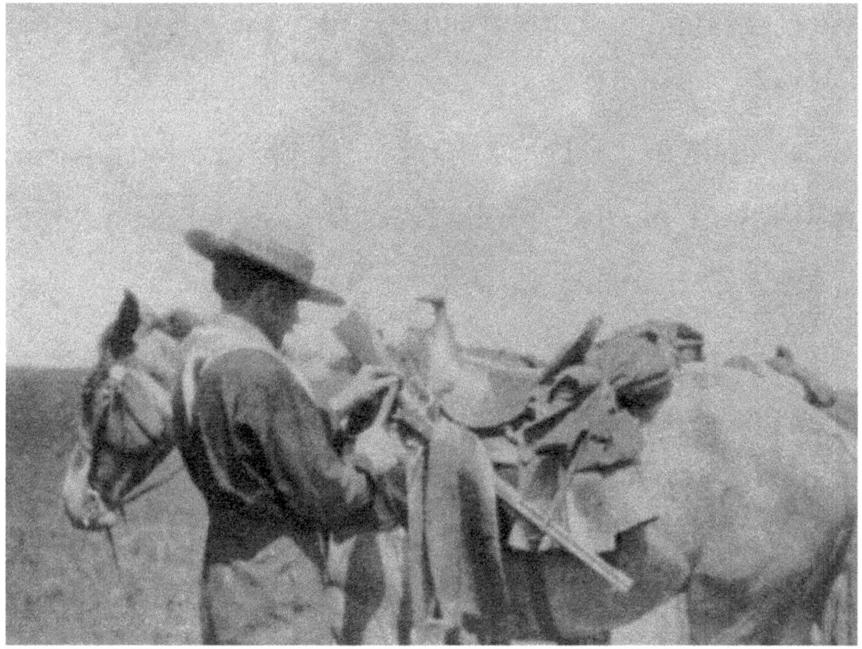

Solon Borglum at home on the plains on his honeymoon at Crow Creek Reservation, 1899. (Photo by unidentified photographer, courtesy of Solon H. Borglum and Borglum family papers, Archives of American Art, Smithsonian Institution.)

Full Circle on the Plains

That morning, Solon and Emma looked out over the reservation and saw 600 tipis stretched out in a great circle across the plains. Emma wrote to family and friends, saying that she saw a great change come over her husband at that moment, as he looked around at the plains and at the Dakota Sioux people.

Emma said she suddenly saw Solon come alive in a way that she had never seen in Paris. He looked as if he were at home with good old friends. She could tell that his life on the plains was what he loved. She told family and friends that, "These things had a mysterious appeal for [Solon], his love for the West's past and hope for its future were keeping a life of its own in his heart."[112]

And although very tired and homesick, Emma took pleasure in the strange and wonderful beauty of their temporary home.[113]

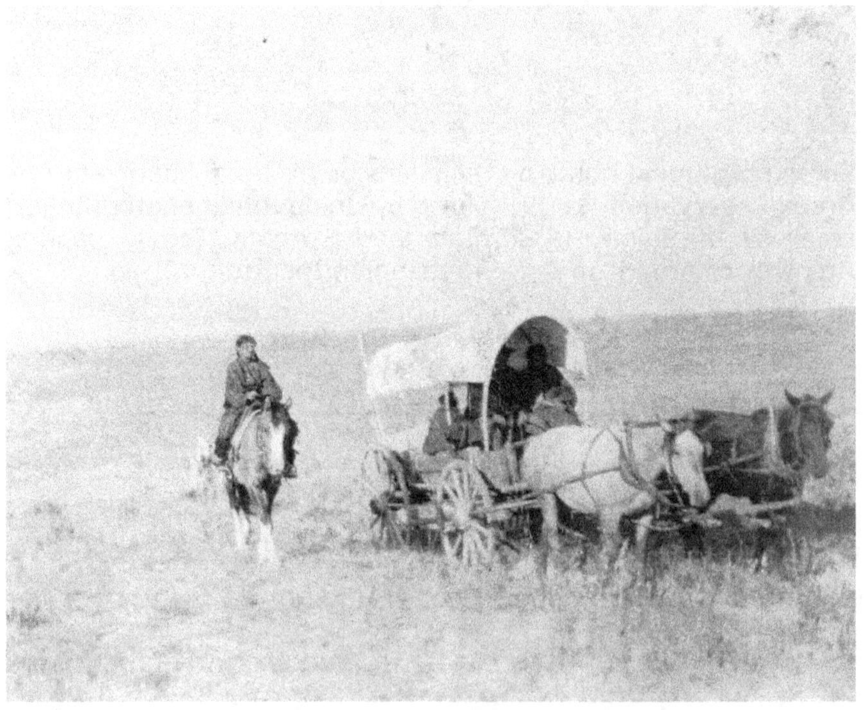

Solon and Emma Borglum (in the covered wagon) while on their honeymoon at Crow Creek Reservation in 1899, with a Native American family. (Photo by unidentified photographer, courtesy of Solon H. Borglum and Borglum family papers, Archives of American Art, Smithsonian Institution.)

South Dakota Adventures

Over the next few months, one of their greatest honeymoon adventures was an eleven-day journey across the plains to Yankton, South Dakota. Solon and Emma traveled in a wagon with a Dakota Indian man named Long Feather and his wife.

The days were hot, and the nights were cold on the plains. The couples traveled by day. Then they made camp and put up a tipi. The four of them slept in the tipi at night, but they had to stay alert day and night, because eagles and coyotes continually tried to steal the meat they had with them. All of that added to their great adventure on the South Dakota plains.[114]

The Buffalo Dance

Another of their great adventures was seeing the Dakota Sioux Buffalo Dance. Solon closely watched and studied the sounds, the sights, and the movements. Afterwards, he began drawing and using what little modeling clay he had with him to try to capture the moment, so he would not forget any of it. (Four years later, he would make a great sculpture of it called *The Sioux Indian Buffalo Dance* for an exhibition.)

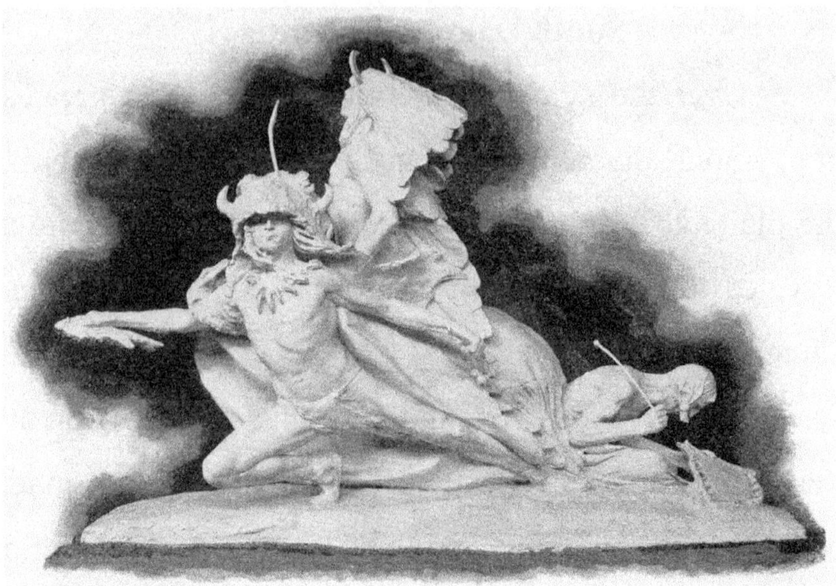

The Sioux Indian Buffalo Dance sculpture by Solon Borglum was inspired by the things he and his bride saw when they lived with the Dakota Sioux people on the Crow Creek Reservation during their 1899 honeymoon in South Dakota. The award-winning sculpture was made four years later. (From a photo of the sculpture in clay by Solon Borglum as printed in a 1904 issue of *The Century* magazine.)

Burial on the Plains

Solon and Emma enjoyed their honeymoon on the South Dakota plains, but bad things happened there too. During that time, a terrible sickness came to the reservation. At least eleven native children died from that illness. Solon helped the Dakota people and helped the missionary with the burial services. From that experience, Solon would later make another of his small white story sculptures called *Burial on the Plains*. (A few years later, Solon and Emma would also suffer the death of a child of their own.)

By the time the honeymooners left the reservation, Emma had learned to love the Dakota Sioux people and their culture almost as much as her husband did. And she was liked by them as well. Many of the things the couple had unsuccessfully tried to buy during the early days of their visit were later given to them, in boxloads, as goodbye gifts, from their Dakota friends.[115]

Solon had brought his bride to the reservation to show her some of the Plains Indian people he loved, and to record their culture and stories through his art. That time with them had been very special for him.

Many good memories and several sculptures would come out of that time on the reservation. During his lifetime, Solon would create about a dozen Native American sculptures and would be known as one of the best sculptors of Native American life in the country.[116] Just like *The Last Roundup* and *Burial on the Plains*, each of those sculptures would have a very personal story to tell.

Chapter 22:
Art and Family

After leaving the reservation, Solon and Emma stopped to visit Solon's family in Omaha. Then the newly-weds traveled east to Washington D.C. to see Emma's brother and to speak to government officials on behalf of the Dakota Sioux people.

But Solon was anxious to return to Paris so he could get to work on his new sculptures. Some of the biggest art exhibitions in the world were asking for him to enter his artworks. Many of those works were later exhibited at the Universal Exposition in Paris in 1900 and the Pan-American Exposition in 1901. There they won major honors and awards. Solon's western art was gaining such a reputation for excellence that he also received a nickname, "The Sculptor of the Prairie."[117]

Family and More Family

In 1900, Solon's stepmother Ida and his youngest sister Harriet came from Omaha to visit him and Emma in Paris. A little later, brother Gutzon, his wife Lisa, and half-brother August Borglum came to visit from London, as well.

Gutzon would visit Solon a few more times after that, but half-brother August would visit Solon often. August, the music scholar from Omaha and London, was actually scheduled to go on to Germany to study music at that time, but he fell in love with Lucy Vignal, Emma's sister, who gave piano recitals in Paris. So August spent much of his time with Solon and the Vignals in France.

Before long, August and Lucy were married. They stayed in Paris so that August could study music. Then they moved to Omaha and opened a music school there.

In the spring of that same year, Solon and Emma's first child was born. Emma had always had servants and had seldom been around children. She had no idea how to care for a baby. But Solon did. He remembered helping his father take care of sick and injured people. He also remembered his ranching days and taking care of newborn calves and colts. Perhaps he remembered helping with younger brothers and sisters at home, too. So when his own first child was born, he quickly picked up his newborn daughter and took charge, showing his nervous wife what to do.

Solon and Emma named their new daughter Lilli. She was a real charmer, and her parents truly adored her.

Chapter 23:
"Sculptor of the Prairie"

When Solon's daughter Lilli was six months old, things changed, and Solon had to go to America on business. The company that provided the metal for his sculptures was in financial trouble and could not supply him with the materials he needed. So his artworks could not be produced for the shows where they were entered.

Western artist Frederick Remington, whose own cowboy sculptures were often compared to Solon's, advised Solon to find a new supplier.[118] But Solon did not have the money and did not know what to do.

That was a time of great patriotism in America, and many people wanted statues made to celebrate local, state, and national heroes. Solon wanted some of those art jobs. But without a studio in America, and without good quality iron and enough money to order it, he could not get the commissions.

Solon was worried. He was stuck in New York. He was not eating right and was often ill. He needed new commissions to stay in business, and he needed money and a studio to do the work. He also needed money to bring his family to America and to take care of them.

But Solon's wife and their second child—a son named Paul—could not wait. Paul was born in Paris in December of 1901. Emma was living with her parents at that time. The delicate woman was worried sick about her husband, but she could not leave her two small children in Paris—and she had no money to send to her husband and no money to go to his side in America.

Solon was then famous as the "Sculptor of the Prairie" in France, but in America, he was far less known—and he had no studio to use. He was forced to take on smaller jobs working for other artists, just to live.

Horses to the Rescue Again

But then, once again, horses came to Solon's rescue. Some other American sculptors had already received commissions to do hero statues. Some of those artists were good at creating figures of people, but they were not as good at making horses look realistic. And most of those statues were of heroes on horseback.

But Solon knew horses. He had created award-winning statues of horses. So he took on some of those jobs to draw and redesign the horses for the hero statues of other artists. That provided him with some money, but it did not bring him much recognition.

Solon was not too proud to work for other artists. And he did not care if people knew he had done parts of those statues. One day, he was completing a model of a horse for another artist while a visitor watched. The visitor complimented his work, saying, "Very good, young man. That horse could even be a Borglum horse."[119] It was! Solon must have laughed quietly at that.

On another day, Solon realized he had designed and sculpted horse statues for two other artists whose hero sculptures were on display at the same time.[120] Solon must have smiled at that, as well.

He must have smiled, too, when he heard he had become so famous in France that he had been admitted to the new National Sculpture Society there. His friend,

Augustus Saint-Gaudens, had sponsored him.[121]

But Solon was still not as well known in New York as in Paris. Saint-Gaudens sent him messages, saying it pained him to hear about his friend Solon's problems in their homeland of America. Saint-Gaudens wrote, "That a man of your talent should be in such a position while men of absolutely no talent and less character have more than they can attend to is deplorable."[122]

More Horses and Cowboys

In New York, Solon kept busy working on the horses for other people's statues. At the same time, he also began to design and model new sculptures of his own, sculptures of horses, cowboys, Plains Indians, and other plainsmen, such as his *Bronco Buster* statue that was sometimes called *One in a Thousand.*

That statue was similar to and often compared to some statues and artwork then being done by two other American cowboy artists, Charles Russell and Frederick Remington. Those two artists had also spent a lot of time in the saddle, riding the range, as cowboys in the Old West. They and Solon used their cowboy and ranch life experiences to tell their stories through their artwork.

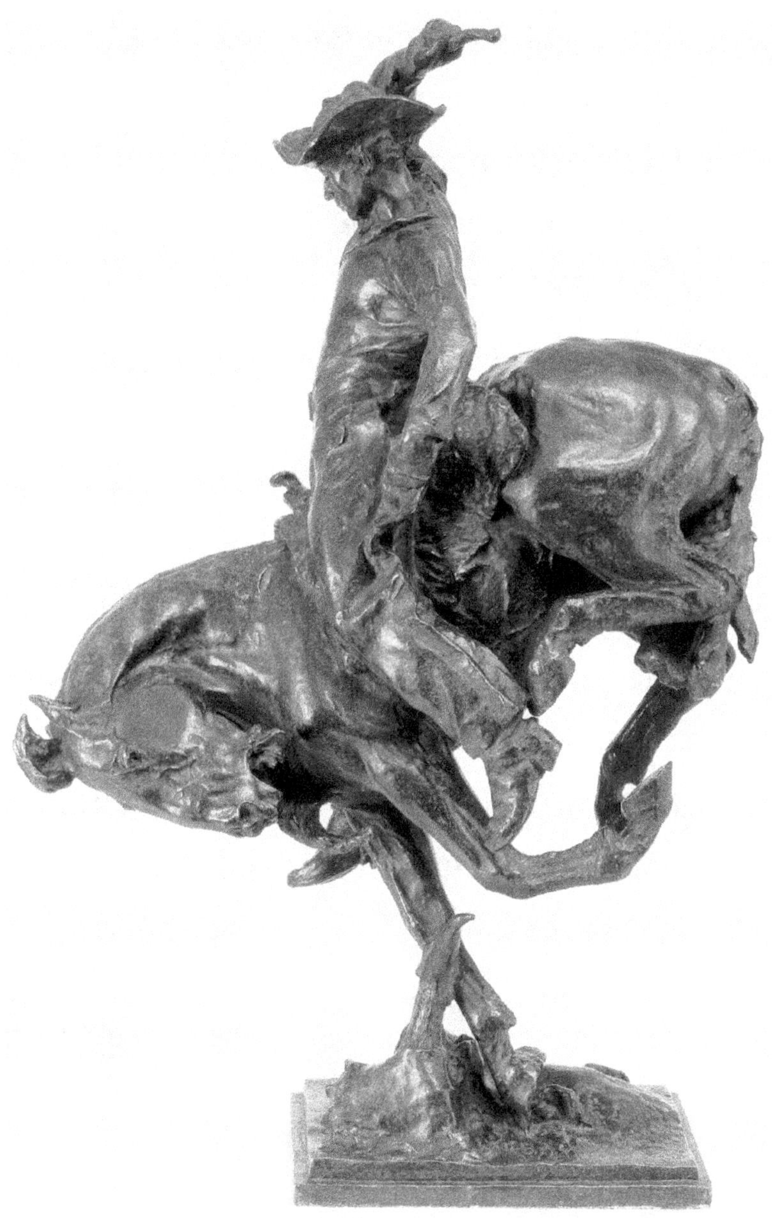

Solon Borglum's *Bronco Buster* sculpture also called *One in a Thousand*. (Photo courtesy, Buffalo Bill Center of the West, Cody Wyoming, U.S.A.; Gertrude Vanderbilt Whitney Trust Fund Purchase, 6.60.)

Advice from a Friend

Saint-Gaudens then advised Solon to ask the St. Louis World's Fair committee if he could enter some of his new plainsmen statues there. The committee not only agreed to that, but also ordered four large sculptures to be displayed at the entrance to the fair. They even gave Solon a large cash advance on his work.

He also had enough money to bring his wife, his two children (Lilli and Paul), and a maid to America. But the French maid was not as happy with the idea as his family was. She left them shortly after setting foot on American soil. Solon then moved his family in to a small boardinghouse in Younkers, New York. Later, he moved them to an apartment house closer to his studio and hired people to help Emma with the house and children.

In the meantime, Solon, who had left his own Nebraska ranch just ten years before, kept busy working on his four new western sculptures for the St. Louis World's Fair. His theme was The Westward Movement of American Civilization.

Those four large sculptures were *Buffalo Dance*, a Native American piece from his honeymoon visit at

Crow Creek; *Pioneer in a Storm*, showing a horse and a man on the prairie; *Cowboy at Rest*, representing ranchers (and perhaps Solon himself on his Nebraska Ranch near Cairo); and *Steps Toward Civilization*, showing a Plains Indian chief encouraging his son to learn the ways of the white people. But Solon would also have nine more sculptures on display there when the world's fair opened in 1904.

Doing Well

For the most part, things seemed to be going well for Solon in the early 1900s. He loved his family dearly and was hard at work—and enjoying it. In April 1903, he even had a one-man show of 32 bronze, marble, and other sculptures. He was becoming well known as a master artist. Newspapers, magazines, and books even called him the "most typically American sculptor."[123]

Several historians and art critics featured him in their books on important American sculptors. One of those was Charles Caffin's book about eleven *American Masters of Sculpture* (that also included Solon's friend Augustus Saint-Gaudens, other friends, and another sculptor named Daniel Chester French).[124]

Soon Solon had more work than he could handle. By then, people were contacting him, wanting him to do horse and hero sculptures of his own. On the surface, things seemed to be going great for him in those early 1900s, but there were many troubles too. During those good times and those times of trouble, he often lost himself in his artwork.

Chapter 24: Family Troubles

By 1903, Solon was one of America's greatest sculptors. But his personal life was starting to fall apart.

His first-born child, his darling daughter Lilli, had always been frail and delicate like her mother Emma. One day, Lilli became ill and died. Both Solon and his wife were grief-stricken.

Not long after that, their second daughter, Monica, was born. But Emma was so depressed that she would have almost nothing to do with her new baby. Solon had to take over as both mother and father for his young children for some time.[125]

Around then, Solon also began facing intense competition and some mistaken identity problems. Much of that involved his older brother Gutzon.[126]

Brotherly Love and Jealousy

At the same time and far away in his own London art world, older brother Gutzon realized that he was no longer happy with his own wife Lisa, or with his old-fashioned painting and drawing style, or with his own reputation, or even as an artist living in Europe. He decided to put away his brushes and pencils and do some sculpting—perhaps because his own younger brother was doing so well with that in France and America.

Gutzon's wife Lisa realized that her husband was getting restless. She also saw that Gutzon was jealous and upset about his brother's fame. She feared her husband would leave her.

She then reminded Gutzon that she was a teacher, and she told him that Solon was only an art student, not an artist. She argued that Solon knew nothing of art. Her words were meant to make Gutzon feel more secure about himself. Instead the words angered her husband and drove him away from her.

Gutzon still loved his "little brother" Solon, but he was also very jealous of him.[127]

Gutzon was an excellent artist, too. He may have

learned the art of sculpting in 1889. He had done some very good sculptures since then. But he had mainly focused on painting and drawing.

Then he had tired of that. He wanted something different, so he left his wife Lisa and went alone to America, taking some of his sculptures with him. He intended to try to get commission work sculpting statues of war heroes, as Solon was already doing. Gutzon even began calling himself "Borglum the Sculptor."[128]

Confusion over "Borglum the Sculptor"

By that time, the art world in America generally knew only one Borglum as a sculptor—and that was Solon. But then Gutzon announced that he was the first and eldest Borglum brother to be a sculptor. He also said that his "little brother" Solon had only been his student.

People were confused by the name similarity and by Gutzon's claims. They did not know what to believe, and at first, Gutzon could not get many sculpting jobs.

Gutzon began to worry. He became so ill that he went to live in his father's house in Omaha to recover. There, he decided to stay in America. He also decided to divorce Lisa.

The Borglum Sculptors

After getting well, Gutzon went to New York where he started his own art studio with his youngest half-sister Harriet as his housekeeper.[129] He then joined some major art organizations and began to exhibit his work at the same shows as Solon. He even called himself “The First Borglum Sculptor” and said he was a Western artist. All of that further confused people in the art world.

Some of Solon’s friends even felt that Gutzon was claiming credit for Solon’s work and talent. One day, a patron reportedly came to Gutzon’s house, asking for “Borglum the Sculptor” (but looking for Solon). Gutzon did not correct the man. Instead Gutzon ended up with a contract to create a sculpture for him. Other people heard about that and thought it was wrong of him to do.

Rather than cause a scandal, Gutzon gave up the contract and resigned from some organizations and shows.[130] But that did not end the confusion. By then, Gutzon was making money and creating his own beautiful sculptures of presidents and war heroes, just as Solon was doing.[131]

The competition between the two artist-brothers

was sometimes fierce. However, Solon, who otherwise would not be bullied, often chose to withdraw from any contest rather than compete against his older brother.

Losing Out

One day Elizabeth "Libby" Custer wanted a statue to honor her late husband General George Custer who had died at the Battle of the Little Big Horn in 1876. She was greatly impressed by some of Solon's works.

Then she saw one of Gutzon's statues and was again impressed by the Borglum name. But she did not realize the artworks were done by two different men. When she met with Gutzon to work out details, he did not tell her that some of those artworks had been done by his brother.

Later, Mrs. Custer announced to her committee that she had found the right artist—Borglum the Sculptor—to do her late husband's statue. When the people asked her which Borglum she meant, she was surprised, confused, and upset. The commission was then given to another sculptor with a different last name.[132] Both Borglum brothers lost out on that competition and others. And that would happen often after that.

Chapter 25:
Losing Lincoln in Lincoln

More and more confusion arose over the two Borglum sculptors. The general public wondered which brother was the real sculptor. Of course, both of them were, but controversy, confusion, and other problems still arose.[133]

Those two very talented brothers found themselves in almost constant competition against each other in most of the important art shows in America and around the world. They also competed for other kinds of sculpting jobs. That was all very frustrating and annoying, and it caused many problems.

Solon tried not to compete against his older brother whenever possible, but Gutzon seemed to enter everything. When Gutzon found that Solon was entered in any competitions, Gutzon would tell everyone that his little brother was just his former student, and that he, Gutzon, had been the first sculptor in the family.

Competing for Lincoln

Older brother Gutzon had done many fine sculptures in America since moving back from London. One of those was a marble head of Abraham Lincoln that had greatly impressed Robert Lincoln (Abraham Lincoln's oldest son). It also impressed President Theodore Roosevelt and others in Washington D.C.

But younger brother Solon was also designing a contest statue of Abraham Lincoln for a different capital city. Solon was making a full-length standing sculpture of Lincoln for the Nebraska State Capitol Building, in Lincoln, Nebraska. That was the capitol building of the state where Gutzon and Solon had grown up.

But Gutzon felt that he should be the one to do that Nebraska statue of Abraham Lincoln instead. So he asked some of his Washington D.C. friends to help him get the job. That led to confusion and arguments within the committee. The chairman then suggested that the two Borglum brothers should do the work together.

The two Borglum brothers were hardly getting along at all at that time, so of course, that would not have worked. As a result, the committee began to look elsewhere for another sculptor to do the job.

Giving Up Lincoln

Realizing he had lost the Nebraska job, Solon wrote a letter, resigning from the Nebraska State Capitol Building competition. Gutzon, too, realized that he had lost what he felt should have been his in the first place, so he also resigned. But Gutzon could not help claiming that the commission should have been his, or perhaps his little brother's, and not someone else's.[134]

Solon never again had the opportunity to do a sculpture of Abraham Lincoln, and Gutzon also lost his chance to do the Lincoln Memorial in Washington D.C., a job he thought he had already won. (But Gutzon would do other statues of Abraham Lincoln, including the Mount Rushmore one a few years after Solon's death.)

Instead, sculptor Daniel Chester French was commissioned to do both statues of Abraham Lincoln—the Nebraska State Capitol statue in Lincoln and the $80,000 Lincoln Memorial statue in Washington, D.C.

Gutzon Borglum was a guest of the governor of Nebraska at a reception on the day Daniel Chester French was announced as the chosen sculptor for the Lincoln (Nebraska) sculpture. There, Gutzon angrily talked about how he thought the situation had been mishandled. He even spoke for his brother Solon, but without Solon's knowledge or permission.[135]

Time For a Change

By then, Solon was tired. He was tired of running up against his brother for jobs and tired of fighting against him in shows and competitions. He was tired of explaining himself and his brother to other people. And he was tired of having to make sculptures for other people. He just wanted to create his own art instead.

He was also tired of living in big cities. He wanted a studio far away, someplace quiet, in the country. He wanted a place where he could work on his own projects and do the artwork that he wanted to do.

He wanted to find land in the country for his home and studio. But he had to stay in the East to get the resources he needed. He would find just what he wanted, at a place called Silvermine, in Connecticut.

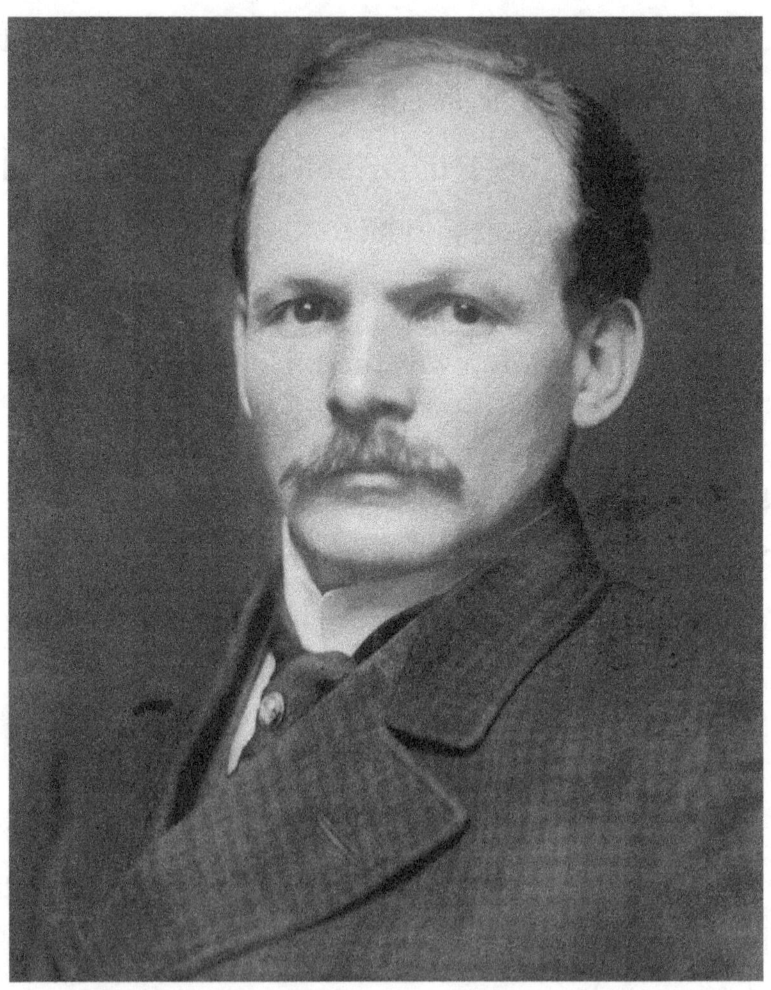

Solon Borglum in the early 1900s. (Hollinger & Co. Photographers. Photo courtesy of Solon H. Borglum and Borglum family papers, Archives of American Art, Smithsonian Institution.)

Chapter 26:
Striking It Rich At Silvermine

Solon stayed busy while he was looking for just the right place for his home and studio. He took part in projects and meetings with various international art associations and committees while many of his statues were being put in places of honor around the country or at the World's Fair. Around that time, he also received a very special and complimentary letter from his good friend Augustus Saint-Gaudens who was dying of cancer.

All of that and more confirmed Solon's decision not only to start fresh, in the country, but to build his new studio on 45 acres of farm land he had found and bought. That land was well away from the big cities. There he could create his own art as he wanted. There he would start an artist colony to help artists teach each other, on land where his two remaining children could grow up unafraid, on land where he could once again have horses.

Solon found what he wanted along the Silvermine River in Connecticut, just 45 miles from New York. Despite its name, it appears there was never any real silver found there. Still it would be a place of rich happiness for Solon.

Home at Rocky Ranch

Solon named his new farm "Rocky Ranch" and built a house, a studio, and a barn there. The property included a creek, fields, hills, and even woods to hike and trails to ride, so he and his family could ride their horses whenever they wanted. He also found and hired Mrs. B., a housekeeper, and her young son Carl. They helped free up both Solon and Emma from many of the day-to-day chores. In that way, Solon and Emma could spend their time enjoying their children and their lives.

Soon a colony of artists came to live in that area. Many of them worked with Solon. They held classes to learn different art methods and styles of art. They held meetings to do constructive criticism to help each other with their art. They also held art exhibits and shows.

Solon and his family even held family and neighborhood get-togethers and history and art programs and pageants. Sometimes they dressed up in their Dakota Sioux clothing and put up their family tipi for others to see and to explore at Rocky Ranch. They also made great friendships with their neighbors.

The Gruelle Family

One of the first artist families to move into the neighborhood near Solon's farm was the Gruelle family (Gru-ELL).[136] It was actually two houses and three generations of Gruelles, with the grandfather Richard, his wife, and their son Justin in one house. In the second house lived another son named Johnny, his wife Myrtle (rhymes with turtle), their young daughter named Marcella Delight, and their baby son named Worth.

Grandfather Gruelle was a minister, and most of his family members were artists or painters of some kind. Johnny Gruelle, one of the adult sons, was also a writer, an illustrator, and a cartoonist for books and magazines.

Solon's daughter Monica and Johnny's daughter Marcella Gruelle were very good friends. They often played together with their dolls in the Silvermine woods.

Elf Tales

Solon loved to see his daughter and the Gruelle girl at play, and he often made up stories to tell them. One of those was about a good little magic elf called Twee-Deedle who could make himself invisible.

In Solon's story, the elf lived in an old apple tree near the Silvermine River. The elf loved to surprise people by making little noises, like the sound of breaking twigs in the woods. As the girls listened to Solon's stories, they even began to think they could see and hear Mr. Twee-Deedle.

Marcella went home and told her father the story. Johnny Gruelle was delighted with the tale. He quickly drew a cartoon of the imaginary elf for his daughter.

Gruelle had been looking for just such an idea to enter in a newspaper contest. He wrote the story, giving Solon credit for the tale, and asked Solon for permission to enter it and the cartoon in the newspaper contest.

Solon gave his permission, and the story of Mr. Twee-Deedle was an instant success. Not only did it win the contest, but it also earned Johnny Gruelle a long-running column in the newspaper.[137]

Missing Marcella

The Borglums and the Gruelles had wonderful times at Silvermine and very sad times too. One day when Marcella Gruelle was about nine, she received a vaccination at school. But when no needle marks showed on her arm, the nurse gave Marcella a second shot.

Not long after that, Marcella became very ill and died. No one knows what killed her, but her parents blamed the vaccine. They and their family were grief-stricken. So were the Borglums, especially Solon's daughter Monica who had lost her playmate.

Despite their grief, Johnny Gruelle and his family continued to live at the Silvermine colony. There he created children's toys and stories to honor the memory of his daughter and her joy of life. Some of his best known creations were a pair of ragdolls, a girl and a boy. Those dolls became known as Raggedy Ann and Andy. Gruelle also wrote a whole series of storybooks about them. Those dolls are now American icons that still delight children and toy collectors today.[138]

Special Neighbors

Many other artists, writers, and businessmen lived

in the Silvermine area and became well known in their own ways, as well. The community was close-knit and rich in culture. But it was much more than just an artist colony.

As W. W. Matthews, a free-lance writer, once said about his Silvermine community, “Our special neighborhood has its literary circles; there are poets and publishers, novelists and art critics. But the pride of our hearts, our own particular joy, is the group of artists who meet every week in the studio-barn of a famous sculptor [Solon Borglum] to compare notes and urge each other on in their delightful work.”[139]

Chapter 27:
A Leader of Boys and Men

Solon Borglum spent a lot of time in his studio or with his family at Silvermine. He created sculptures of American heroes and read about American history. But he closely watched what was going on in Europe, too.

He had heard about a boys' organization in England that was just starting up in the United States in 1910. Here it was called the Boy Scouts of America. He thought it was a wonderful organization, so in 1911, he became a scout leader for his son Paul and for many other boys and young men in the Silvermine area.[140]

The Boy Scout creed matched well with Solon's own personal philosophy of honor, integrity, resourcefulness, and hard work. It also matched up with his lifetime love of nature, hiking, camping, trailcraft, and outdoor life. He was good at all those things, and doing those things helped him stay in great shape as he got older. He had much to teach the boys and others too.

Wars

During those years, Solon also realized that a war was coming, and he knew it would be a big one—The Great War, The World War, or "The War To End All Wars" (even though it did not)—a war now known as World War I (or World War One).

About the time World War I was rising on the international horizon, the small war between the Borglum brothers was ending. Just a few years after Solon bought Rocky Ranch, at Silvermine, Connecticut, Gutzon and his new wife Mary bought 200 acres of farmland not far away, near Stamford, Connecticut. Gutzon named his own place Borgland.

Instead of causing problems, the nearness of the two brothers and their families actually led to a new friendship, respect, and peace between them. Solon, Gutzon, and their families became very close. The two brothers even began working on some related art projects.

Final Projects

In 1918, Solon was busy sculpting three big works that were spiritual or religious in nature. Two of those were large Native American companion pieces that stood looking up to the heavens as if in personal prayer. He called them *Aspiration* and *Inspiration.*

They stood nine feet tall, and they were roughly finished. They probably looked very similar to Solon's very first original Plains Indian carvings on the sandhills bluffs near his Loup River ranch in Nebraska. In some ways, his artwork had come full circle, back to where it had started.

His other artwork was a creation piece called *The Heavens.* It was one part of a four-artist, four-piece project begun by Solon, Gutzon, and two other unrelated artists. The two Borglum brothers were the only two artists to complete their pieces. Solon's *The Heavens* was finished for that project before he left for World War I, but somehow that artwork has since been lost.[141]

Chapter 28:
"Of Some Use in the War"

Once America became involved in the Great War (World War I) in Europe in 1917, Solon could no longer work on his art. He wrote in his war diary, saying, "When we entered this great war, my sole wish in life was to get in and help. To go on with my sculpture was impossible." He was almost 50 years old—too old to be a soldier. He was teaching art twice a week and drilling as a soldier with the home guard in Connecticut, but he wanted to do more—in Europe.[142]

Then a friend told him that the YMCA was looking for older men to go overseas with the American troops, to help soldiers from several countries deal with whatever problems they had. In those days, the YMCA was somewhat different than today.

Like the Boy Scouts, the YMCA had started in England. For a long time, it was an organization that helped men in the big cities find places to stay and to get help when they needed it. But the YMCA also helped greatly with America's and Europe's war efforts.

Solon applied for and was accepted as a YMCA worker for overseas duty. He then wrote in his diary, "I am exceedingly happy that I am going to be of some use in this war."[143]

Food and Comfort

Solon was then sent to France where most of the fighting was going on. His wife still had family there, and he spoke a little French. At first, he was in charge of a building where French soldiers were sent to rest and recover from the fighting, but more and more he was sent closer to the war.

Wherever they sent him, Solon tried to talk to the soldiers in their own language. He did not stay back in the safe areas. Instead, he followed not far behind the soldiers as they moved forward into battle. When they stopped for the night, he moved up. He set up places for them to rest and helped them find shelter and comfort.

He also provided them with coffee, sandwiches, cigarettes, cigars, candy, or whatever he had. In a letter home to Emma, he said his heart was very happy, as he passed out "cups of coffee and chocolate to the weary soldiers returning from the front: Australians, French, British, Senegalese, Tunisians, Algerians, Canadians, and black and white Americans."[144]

Recognizing "The American"

Solon treated all of those soldiers as heroes and friends and did whatever work needed to be done, no matter whose job it was or what it cost him. The soldiers appreciated and respected him for all that.[145] Whatever he did boosted their morale and made them feel less lonesome. And soon they began to recognize him. They smiled and respectfully called him "The American" in French, whenever they saw him.

Solon wanted to move more freely with the French troops and wanted to be allowed up near the front lines with them. Finally, he and one helper were given permission to go where they wanted. They moved with and among the soldiers, and they always tried to have hot coffee available for them, wherever they went.

Solon wore a French uniform but he was not a soldier, so he used no gun to protect himself. But that did not stop him from suffering the effects of three deadly gas attacks, the kind that destroyed men's lungs and killed many soldiers in that war.

By the time that war was over, Solon's uniform was ragged, his lungs were not healthy, and he was exhausted. But he was glad he had been able to help. And the soldiers loved and respected him for all his efforts.

After the war was over, and before the French soldiers were allowed to go home, they had to establish order and new laws and government rules over Germany. At that time, Solon was busy overseeing several YMCA centers over a very large area. He was also having trouble getting from one place to another.

To Solon's delight, one of the officers gave him a horse to ride, to get around faster and better. That helped, but like the French soldiers, Solon was getting anxious to be home with his family. He wanted to be back home in time for Christmas.

The Christmas Party

Then Solon realized that the French soldiers would

not be home with their families for Christmas either. So he decided to hold a big American Christmas party for his many new friends. He wanted to hold a party for a whole regiment of French soldiers, more than 1,600 men. He even went looking for presents for all of them, nothing big, just pocket knives, pipes, tobacco pouches, chocolate bars, or whatever he could find—at least one gift for each man—and he paid for those gifts himself.

By his 50th birthday, December 22, 1918, Solon had it all put together, 1,750 presents—small gifts, but very much appreciated. Then, he had four Christmas trees set up for the celebration.

What an awesome Christmas that must have been for the French soldiers! They had been away from home and fighting in a war for many years, long before the Americans joined in on their side to help them finish that war! The soldiers greatly enjoyed their Christmas party.

Honoring "The American"

Days later, during a New Year's celebration, the French troops were called together to hear a speech from a French soldier who had been a German prisoner of war. That Frenchman told of the hardships of war and of being a prisoner. He talked about one man, in particular, a man who had had a major impact on his life since then. He said that man was an American volunteer, a man who did not have to be there, but was! He said that man was the first American to enter French battlefields when the battles were over.[146] He was an American who had earned the Frenchman's greatest respect and appreciation.

Honoring the Man

Then Solon heard his own nickname called in French, "The American." The French officers and soldiers clapped their hands and pushed Solon forward.

The French colonel pinned a medal on Solon's chest, grabbed both of his shoulders, and kissed both sides of his face. That was a typical French custom. Solon was so surprised and embarrassed—and overwhelmed. Then a band played both the French and the American national anthems, one after the other.

At that point, Solon realized what the colonel had said. Solon had been awarded the Croix de Guerre (kwah duh gare), the French Cross of War, one of the highest honors a French military man could receive. But Solon was not a French soldier. He was an American volunteer.

The French government knew that. Still they had awarded him one of France's highest military honors (a French medal similar to America's Congressional Medal of Honor). The French colonel also sent a letter home to Solon's wife to tell her that Solon was tired—but doing well—and that he was very much appreciated![147]

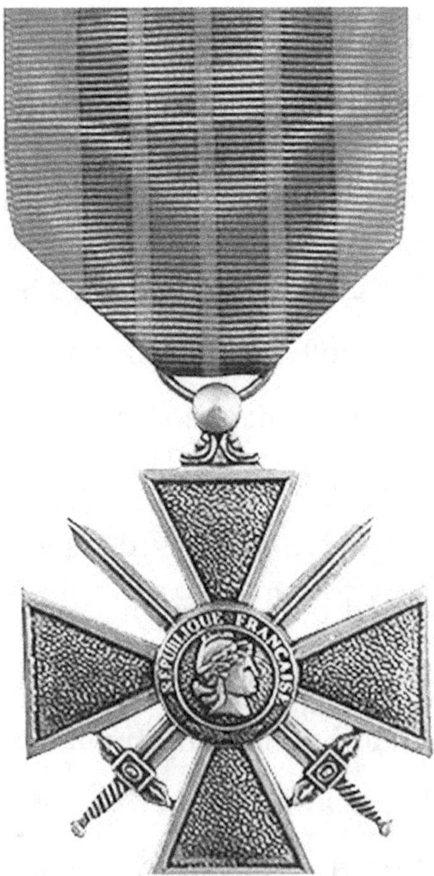

The French Croix de Guerre (Cross of War) War Medal, similar to the one given to Solon Borglum by the French for his efforts toward the French soldiers and their allies in World War I.

Chapter 29:
Home from the War

While serving in France, Solon kept a war journal. It contained many entries and thirteen pencil and ink sketches he made during the war. Before Solon could leave France for home, someone borrowed that diary, and returned it to him with over a hundred signatures and messages of thanks from people whose lives he had touched—Frenchmen, Americans, Belgians, and many others—civilians and soldiers.

After the war, Solon and the American soldiers in France waited to go home. But it would take months to process their paperwork and transfer them back. In the meantime, they had to find something to do to stay out of trouble in Paris. Solon wondered what he could do to help his countrymen? Before long, he had the answer.

Another Nebraska Leader

During World War I, the American Army in Europe was known as the American Expeditionary Force or the A.E.F. That army was under the direction of another Nebraskan, a man named General John J. Pershing. Pershing was born in Missouri, but he had lived and served at army forts in Nebraska and South Dakota. Pershing also taught mathematics and military science at the University of Nebraska in Lincoln.

One of Pershing's officers, Major George Gray, had an idea about what to do with the American soldiers who were waiting to go home from France. Gray said,

> Our army of citizen-soldiers found itself at the end of the [war] in [France on] a foreign land which is a…treasure house of art of every description, whose history is…laced with the history of art, a land which for ages has been producing masters and masterworks, a land [of] …museums, schools, and instructors of great gifts.[148]

Gray's idea was to make those art resources available to artist-soldiers who wanted to learn about them. One of those instructors would be Solon Borglum, who had chosen to stay and help instead of going home. Other art instructors would also be American or French artists.

The A.E.F. Art School

With the aid of the French government, the new one-building A.E.F. School of Fine Arts for Advanced Students opened its temporary doors near Paris on March 15, 1919. Solon was appointed head of the Sculpture Department. He was given the rank of honorary captain.

He had 16 soldier-students working with him. All were advanced artists eager to trade their weapons of war for their choice of art supplies and access to wonderful facilities and master mentors and teachers.

And Solon loved it as well. In between teaching and mentoring, he toured Paris and its museums. He made sketches of buildings, especially cathedrals, and worked on art projects to bring home with him.

Just three months after opening its doors, the A.E.F. School of Fine Arts for Advanced Students closed its doors on June 15, 1919. That was when the last of its American soldier-students left France to go home. The school had served its purpose. Solon was very pleased and proud to have been a part of that great experiment.

Home from the War

By then, Solon had been at war and away from home for just over a year, but when he returned home, he noticed that many things had changed. All of America seemed to be moving at a much faster pace. The towns in America seemed bigger and busier, and automobiles (not horses) took people places.

Solon's family and life at Silvermine had changed, too. Everyone was glad to welcome him home. But his family seemed far more independent. His wife had worked away from home as a teacher while he was gone, and his children had grown up. Paul had graduated from high school, and Monica was becoming a young woman.

Solon worried about his children's education and their future. He urged them to learn more about the world and to graduate from college. He often wished that he had had more education himself.

Many things had changed during the war, even Solon himself. He still wanted to sculpt and teach, but he also wanted to write. Brother August agreed to help him organize his notes for some books and magazine articles.

Doing Too Much

Six months after coming home, Solon also opened The School of American Sculpture in New York. He hoped that the new school would become another A.E.F.-sponsored college of art. That did not happen, but the school did grow, and it became well-known.

By 1921, Solon was spending much of his time moving between his home studio in Connecticut and his School of American Sculpture in New York. He was trying to run them both. He had never had a head for business, and he never had enough time for his art. He was also spending as much time as possible with his family, as well as writing, lecturing, and setting up exhibits while working on many projects.

He was trying to do too much, and he was beginning to feel the stress and strain.

Chapter 30:
End of the Trail

In January 1922, Solon began to suffer severe migraine headaches and serious stomach pains. He blamed his illnesses on overwork and tried to ignore them. But they would not go away. A doctor came to see him at Rocky Ranch, but Solon just got worse.

A few days later, he was hospitalized. Only then did the doctors realize that his appendix had burst. There were no antibiotics or wonder drugs in those days. Medicine was limited, and appendicitis could be deadly.

The doctors operated, and Solon came out of the operation well. Despite his bad lungs, he was still fairly strong, and the doctors expected him to recover.

He even seemed much better the next day, so only his wife Emma and his brother Gutzon were at his bedside. But the following day, Solon was worse. His children were called to the hospital, but his son Paul was away at college and could not make it home right away. Brother Gutzon had been asked not to come back, because the family was afraid he would upset Solon.[149]

Grief and Disbelief

Solon was sleeping very soundly on the afternoon of January 30, 1922, when a nurse told his wife and daughter to leave the room and go for a walk.

While they were gone, older brother Gutzon walked into the hospital room, calling out to Solon in a loud and cheery voice that it was time to wake up. Gutzon announced that the two Borglum brothers still had great sculpture projects to do together.

But Gutzon's loud voice could not wake his brother. Solon could not and would not wake up. Gutzon cried out for his little brother and for all the time they had lost.

Gutzon made so much noise that Solon's daughter Monica heard him and ran back into the room. She lost control and told her uncle that it was too late. She said that he should have told her father how he felt about him while Solon was awake and could hear him. At that, Gutzon turned silent and ran from the hospital room.[150]

Solon Borglum would never wake up again. He died a few hours later, just nine days after he first became ill. His death was the result of complications from a burst appendix. But there were other factors too, including worry, overwork, exhaustion, severe headaches, indigestion problems, and the World War I gas damage to his lungs. It had all been too much for his body. He had just turned 53 years old, and no one could believe that such a strong, heroic, and wonderfully talented man was suddenly gone.[151]

The Funeral

Solon's funeral was held in his Rocky Ranch studio at Silvermine, among his current sculptures, his tools, his artist smock and apron, his French YMCA uniform and medal of war, his wife's portrait, and other things he knew and loved. Inside the studio, there was hardly room for his many mourners—family, friends, neighbors, artists, students, and more—who had come, in grief and disbelief, to say their goodbyes and to praise him.

Brother Gutzon drove his own wife Mary to the funeral in a horse-drawn wagon, but Gutzon either could not or would not go inside for the funeral.[152] He grieved alone. Later, he would write a letter to the *New York Times* praising Solon highly for his work and for the way he had lived his life. In that editorial, Gutzon compared his younger brother to his art, using the words of one of Solon's students who said Solon had been "big, simple, true, and real, [and] presided over by a rare and great spirit."[153]

Aspiration* and *Inspiration

The funeral service was also presided over by two of Solon's last sculptures, ones that had been created for placement in a church.[154] They were copies of his nine-foot tall Native American statues known as *Aspiration* and *Inspiration*. They had been moved across his studio to take their place beside his coffin for his funeral.

Roughly made, but tall and stately, those two Native American figures seemed to stand guard and stand in tribute and prayer. With their faces lifted toward the light coming in through the high windows from the heavens, those figures seemed to be paying their respects to the great spirit of their own maker, Solon Borglum, the "Sculptor of the Prairie," a man who had also loved and often paid great tribute to Native American cultures.

After the funeral, Solon Borglum was laid to rest nearby, in the neighborhood cemetery there at Silvermine, Connecticut, near his own much beloved Rocky Ranch.

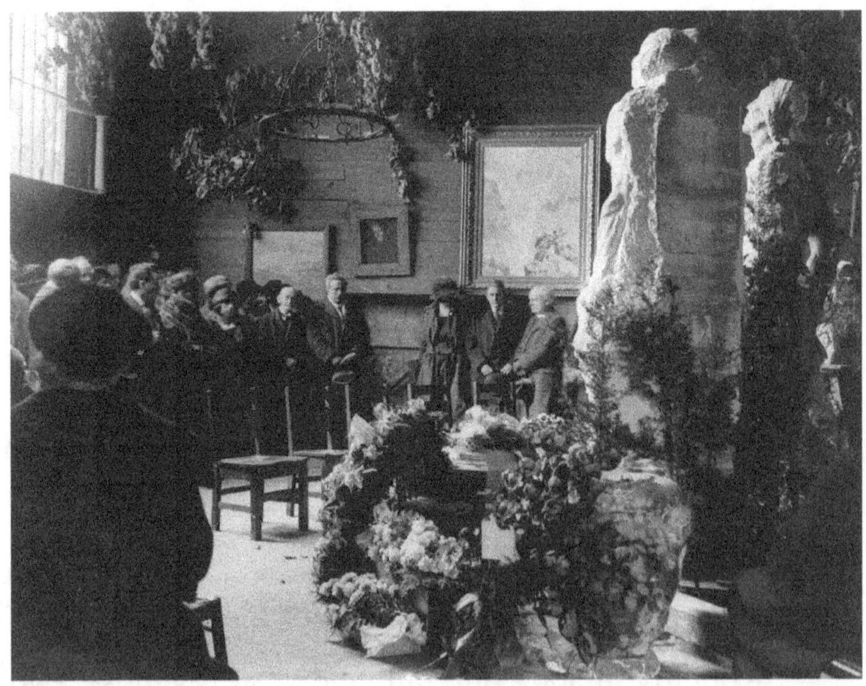

Solon Borglum's funeral, in his studio, 1922, coffin covered with flowers (center). To the right are his two (9 foot tall) Native American statues, *Aspiration* and *Inspiration*, with faces uplifted, toward the light from a window. (Photo by unidentified photographer, courtesy of Solon H. Borglum and Borglum family papers, Archives of American Art, Smithsonian Institution.)

Chapter 31:
In the Shadows

In 1935, thirteen years after Solon Borglum's death, the editors of the *Omaha World-Herald* newspaper asked a state college administrator and two university history professors the following question: [If we had] a Nebraska Hall of Fame, who should be in it?[155]

Each of those educators then developed a list of 20 famous but no-longer-living Nebraskans who they felt deserved to be in the Hall of Fame. Their lists were combined and re-ranked. The 6th name on the final list of 20 suggested honorees was that of Solon Borglum.

In 1935, there was not yet a Nebraska Hall of Fame—just the possibility of one. Today there is such a Hall, located in the Nebraska State Capitol Building. But Solon Borglum is not yet a member of that Hall of Fame.

Today, few people even know who Solon Borglum was or why he should be honored there. Today he is nearly forgotten—almost a secret again.

A Lasting Legacy

Western writer Louis L'Amour once wrote that, "It is this by which we measure a man, by what he does with his life, by what he creates to leave behind." If that is so, then Solon Borglum was indeed a great man.

During his relatively short lifetime, Solon Hannibal Borglum mentored and helped many people from many different countries and created wonderful works of art to leave behind as his legacy. As a sculptor, he created at least 80 Old West story sculptures and more than 55 other American hero monuments in plaster, marble, bronze, wood, and other materials, as well as several copies of each of those. He also created other artworks that were given away as gifts or sold for living expenses during his early years.

Fortunately, Solon's art is still well represented in galleries and museums around the world, including one piece called *Our Slave*, at the Joslyn Art Museum, in Omaha where he had lived. He has been ranked by art experts as one of the best western artists of the Old West, along with the better known Frederick Remington and Charles Russell, with whom he was often compared.[156]

Although few people today remember Solon's name and accomplishments, many do know of his older brother John Gutzon Borglum and Gutzon's biggest claim to fame, Mount Rushmore. That memorial was started in 1925, just three years after Solon's death. As a result, Solon's accomplishments are often lost or forgotten in the shadow of his brother's work. But just think of what those two brothers might have been able to do if they had ever carved together—as they intended.

Inspiration

Many people believe Solon's Plains Indian carvings on the bluff near the Borglum Ranch in Nebraska inspired his brother Gutzon to try his own hand at sculpting.[157] Some also believe that Solon's early death may have inspired Gutzon to take on his own greatest challenge—the carving of Mount Rushmore.

Solon did not live to see the start of Mount Rushmore, his brother's crowning achievement. Even Gutzon did not live to see the monument completed. His son Lincoln had to finish it for him.

Solon and Gutzon are both gone, but their Borglum name lives on, in carvings, in art, and in legends—across the prairies and plains, across America, and around the world. They were men who carved sand, stone, clay, iron, wood, and more, and they left a deep impression on the land and on people who knew them.

How proud their Danish woodcarver father, James (Jens) Borglum, would have been of his two once-secret sons Solon and Gutzon, who would never have been born if their parents had not been Mormons.

Tribute to "The Sculptor of the Prairie"

As adults, both of those brothers were sometimes called "Borglum the Sculptor," and Solon was called "The Sculptor of the Prairie." The Nebraska prairie and plains were his proving ground, his subject, his canvas, his inspiration, his love, and his claim to fame. And he was truly a cowboy, a rancher, a sheriff, and a student of history and art there.

So, it seems fitting that someday Solon might be inducted into the Nebraska Hall of Fame. If so, a bust sculpture of him will be created by another sculptor, and that likeness will take its place in the Nebraska Capitol's Hall of Fame along with other Nebraskans of excellent character. That would be a great and fitting tribute to Solon Borglum, "The Sculptor of the Prairie" and plains, a man who told Old West stories in stone, a man who did sculptures of other great men, a man who inspired other artists (even his own older brother), and a man who even inspired World War I soldiers—men of many different nationalities, including the French who awarded him their own Croix de Guerre or Cross of War medal.

Beyond that, Solon was a teacher and role model. He loved art and history, and he respected people of all ethnicities, cultures, and ages. He proved his worth in peace and in war, in his own country and in Europe, and he won the hearts and honors of those who knew him.

Once, Solon Borglum was a secret son who grew up in Nebraska to become a well-known legend of the plains. Now he is almost forgotten again. But his story is well worth knowing and telling. He contributed greatly to the world, and he is a man who should be remembered for many good things, especially in Nebraska, one of the states where he grew up and learned to be a good man.

Chapter 32:
Afterword: The Historical Marker

If you ever travel Nebraska Highway 2—one of Nebraska's Scenic Highways and Byways—toward the Black Hills and Mount Rushmore, you might someday see a historical marker on the side of the road, a few miles west of Cairo, Nebraska. It may be near the old Borglum Ranch site, and it may even point to the sandhills bluffs where Solon Borglum carved his first monumental figure of a Plains Indian—that carving that may have inspired Solon's brother Gutzon to become a monumental landscape sculptor, too.

As such, that Solon Borglum trail marker may also point out the place where Solon, the Nebraska rancher who was the likely inspiration for his own statue of *Cowboy at Rest*, looked out over the land he loved. From there, that Borglum trail marker may also point the way along Nebraska Highway 2 toward Mount Rushmore in South Dakota, the place where Solon's older brother Gutzon continued that legacy by carving out an American iconic shrine to four of our country's greatest presidents.

If and when such a trail marker is put in place for Solon, it will be there through the efforts and through the gifts of those who admired Solon Borglum and loved his work—and loved, too, the lands, the cultures, and the history of Nebraska, the Old West, and America that Solon also loved and worked so hard to show and tell.

Thinking More About Solon Borglum: Suggested (Optional) Questions and Activities

1. Make a list of some positive character traits that describe Solon Borglum. Choose the one you think best describes him and tell why you chose that one. Compare with someone else's choice.
2. Use a print or internet version of the *Nebraska Blue Book* (the official state book of Nebraska) or other source to research the Nebraska Hall of Fame and its current members. Share your findings with classmates. Or look up Hall of Fame people from another state.
3. Write a letter to a state government official or newspaper detailing why you think Solon Borglum or some other person from your state should be inducted into the Hall of Fame.
4. Imagine yourself as Solon Borglum, living as a secret son, not because your family has done anything wrong, but because their religion and/or the laws have changed. How might you feel about that? Write about those feelings and/or create artworks to show them.
5. Even today there are many religions, societies, or nations that have different restrictions. Imagine you are a member of one of those. Research that lifestyle and write about how your life might have been different than it is today.
6. Make a map showing the different places that Solon and his family members have lived.
7. Research your own family history and family names.
8. Lifestyles, mortality rates, health, schooling, and much more were very different in the 1800s and early 1900s. Pick one of those aspects of life and research or discuss how and why it might have been different than today.
9. How did Solon Borglum's love of horses, Native Americans, cowboys, or the Old West influence his art talents?
10. From the book or other research, discuss the longtime relationship Solon had with his full brother John Gutzon, or with his half-brothers Arnold or August.
11. Why didn't the Borglum Ranch do well in Nebraska in the 1880s?
12. How did the Borglums' California ranch and/or their Nebraska ranch influence what Solon did with his life?

13. How did Solon feel about Native Americans? How do you know that from the book? Give examples to prove your ideas.
14. Who or what was most responsible for Solon's great talents and accomplishments in art? Defend your answer.
15. How would you describe Solon's quest to become an artist? What drove or motivated him? How did he know where he needed to go or what he needed to do?
16. Whenever Solon was lonely or feeling lost, he always found himself drawn to something he loved. What? Show examples.
17. What was the background of Solon's wife Emma and how well did she seem to fit into his life and his love of art?
18. Of all the things Solon did in his life, what do you think was his most remarkable or worthy achievement? Why?
19. Research the early history, mission statement, and role of the YMCA (Young Men's Christian Association) and describe how it may have changed since its early history.
20. Compare the French Croix de Guerre medal to the American Congressional Medal of Honor. Why did the French give Solon the Croix de Guerre, and why was that so unusual?
21. In what ways do you think Gutzon inspired Solon and his art? In what ways do you think Solon inspired Gutzon?
22. Many of solon's artworks were actually true stories of his life experiences while ranching. Describe one or more of those from the story or find a picture of one of his artworks and tell what the story might have been about.
23. Do you think it was appropriate that Solon's brother Gutzon called himself "Borglum the Sculptor" when he came back to America? Why or why not? Do you think it is appropriate now?
24. Compare some of Solon Borglum's Old West art to artworks by Charles Russell or Frederick Remington (paintings, drawings, or sculptures). How are they similar, and how are they different? Which one(s) do you like better and why?
25. Do you think the nickname "Sculptor of the Prairie" was a good nickname for Solon Borglum? Why or why not? If not, who do you think deserved that nickname?
26. The title of this book is *Secret Brother*. In what ways could that term describe Solon Borglum?
27. Another possible title for this book was *In the Shadow of Mount Rushmore*. How might that title have referred to Solon?

Selected Bibliography

Teaching Resources:

Along Nebraska Pioneer Trails. Educational Leaflet No. 12. Lincoln: Nebraska State Historical Society. N.d. Available from http://www.usgennet.org/usa/ne/topic/resources/NSHS/EDLFT/edlft12.html

Nebraska Trailblazers #1 Native Americans, #3 Oregon Trail, #5 Settlers' Homes, #8 Ranching, #10 Railroads, #16 Red Cloud and the Sioux Nation. Nebraska State Historical Society. Available at http://www.nebraskahistory.org/museum/teachers/material/trailist.htm

Nonfiction:

1864 Emigration. Mormon Trails Organization, website, http://www.mormontrails.org/Trails/Yearly/1864.htm

Along Nebraska Pioneer Trails. Educational Leaflet No. 12. Lincoln: Nebraska State Historical Society. N.d. Available from http://www.usgennet.org/usa/ne/topic/resources/NSHS/EDLFT/edlft12.html

Armstrong, Selene Ayer. "Solon H. Borglum: Sculptor of American Life: An Artist Who Knows the Value of 'Our Incomparable Materials,'" *The Craftsman,* July 1907, Vol. 12, pp. 382-389. [See *Highlights in the Life of Solon H. Borglum, Sculptor, 1868-1922.*]

Bagley, Will. *South Pass: Gateway to a Continent.* Norman, OK: University of Oklahoma Press, 2014.

Bartels, Alan J. "Prairie Sculptors," *Nebraska Life Magazine.* September/October 2012. (Also http://www.nebraskalife.com/Prarie-Sculptors/) [sic]

Blackman, E. E. "Report of Archeologist 1907," *Proceedings and Collections of the Nebraska State Historical Society,* Volume 15, Nebraska State Historical Society Publications, Series II, Volume X, Jacob North Co., 1907.

"Borglum Gets War Cross," *American Art News,* Feb. 8, 1919, p. 1. [See *Highlights in the Life of Solon H. Borglum,* Sculptor, *1868-1922.*]

Boye, Alan. The Complete Roadside Guide to Nebraska. 2nd Ed. Lincoln, NE: University of Nebraska Press, 1989, 2007, p. 187.

Breinholt, J. C. L. *Autobiography* (formerly in Msd 2050), p. 10, 12. LDS Church Historical Department Archives. http://user.xmission.com/~nelsonb/voyage_desc.htm#monarch

Caffin, Charles H. Chapter X "Solon Hannibal Borglum," in *American Masters of Sculpture: Being Brief Appreciations of Some American Sculptors and of Some Phases of Sculpture in America.* New York: Doubleday, Page & Co., 1913.

Carter, Kate B. ed. *Our Pioneer Heritage*, Vol 8. "Scandinavian Immigration – 1864" Salt Lake City: Daughters of Utah Pioneers, 1965. pp. 23-31. http://user.xmission.com/~nelsonb/scand64.htm

Casey, Robert J. and Mary Borglum. *Give the Man Room: The Story of Gutzon Borglum.* NY: Bobbs-Merrill, 1952.

Davies, A. Mervyn. Solon H. Borglum: *A Man Who Stands Alone.* Chester, CT:

Pequot Press, 1974.

"Drake's Account of Borglum Family Verified," and "On the Side," Cairo Record, Nov(?) 1963 (clippings from the Cairo Roots Museum archives).

Eberle, Louise. "In Recognition of an American Sculpture," *Scribner's Magazine*, July–Sept 1922, Vol. 72, pp. 379-384. [See *Highlights in the Life of Solon H. Borglum, Sculptor, 1868-1922.*]

[Editorial] *Grand Island Independent*, January 20, 1908.

Falk, Peter H. ed. "Solon H(annibal) Borglum." *Who Was Who in American Art*. Sound View Press, 1985. p. 66.

Geske, Norman A. "Solon Hannibal Borglum." *Art and Artists in Nebraska*. Lincoln: Sheldon Memorial Art Gallery, University of Nebraska, 1989. p. 31.

Goodrich, Arthur. "The Frontier in Sculpture," *Denver Times*. Vol. 33 #26, March 7, 1903. [See *Highlights in the Life of Solon H. Borglum, Sculptor, 1868-1922.*]

[Graff, Jane]. *Virtual Nebraska: Nebraska...Our Towns: Cairo-Hall County*. At www.casde.unl.edu/history/counties/hall/cairo.

Hall, Patricia. *Johnny Gruelle: Creator of Raggedy Ann and Andy*. Gretna, LA: Pelican Publishing Co., 1993.

Hassrick, Peter H. "Solon Borglum: Poet Sculptor of the West," in *Shaping the West: American Sculptors of the 19th Century*. Western Passages series. Denver, CO: Petrie Institute of Western American Art, Denver Art Museum, 2010. Pages 26-53.

Highlights in the Life of Solon H. Borglum, Sculptor, 1868-1922 [Book of many newspaper and magazine clippings and handwritten items about Solon Borglum, presented to the Nebraska State Historical Society by his children Paul A. Borglum and Monica Borglum Davies], 1965.

"Jan 9, 1887: Record Cold and Snow Decimates Cattle Herds," *This Day in History* [History.com website]. Available at http://www.history.com/this-day-in-history/record-cold-and-snow-decimates-cattle-herds

"Jan 12, 1888: Blizzard Brings Tragedy to Northwest Plains," *This Day in History*. [History.com website]. Available at http://www.history.com/this-day-in-history/blizzard-brings-tragedy-to-northwest-plains

Kimball, Stanley B. *Mormon Trail Network in Nebraska, 1846-1868: A New Look.* BYU Studies. Salt Lake City: BYU, 1984.

Lamar, Howard R. ed. "Solon Hannibal Borglum." *The Readers Encyclopedia of the American West.* Crowell, 1977. p. 115.

Mapes, Charles Boyd. *The Nebraska City-Fort Kearny Cut-Off as a Factor in the Early Development of Nebraska and the West.* [Masters Thesis] Lincoln: University of Nebraska-Lincoln, 1931. Available from http://digitalcommons.unl.edu/historydiss/20/

Memories of St. Michael, Nebraska 1886-1986. St. Michael Centennial Committee, St. Michael, Nebraska, 1986.

"Mr. Borglum's Broncos and Bronco-Busters," *Harper's Weekly*, May 16, 1903, Vol. 47, p. 790. [See *Highlights in the Life of Solon H. Borglum, Sculptor, 1868-1922.*]

Mormon Trail, Mormon Trails Organization. Available at

http://cdrh.unl.edu/diggingin/trailsummaries/di.sum.0006.html

Moulton, Candy. Roadside History of Nebraska. Missoula, MT: Mountain Press Publishing Co., 1997, p. 385.

Nebraska City Cutoff, 1864-1967. Available from http://www.mormontrails.org/Trails/Variants/NebraskaCity/wyomingvar.htm

"Nebraska City/Ft. Kearney [sic] Cut-Off," *Digging In: The Historic Trails of Nebraska.* Available from http://cdrh.unl.edu/diggingin/historicimages/index.html

Nebraska Hall of Fame, Nebraska State Historical Society, Dec 2000. http://www.nebraskahistory.org/publish/publicat/timeline/nebraska_hall_of_fame.htm

"Nebraska Sculptor, World-Famous," *World Herald*, April 12, 1903. See *Highlights in the Life of Solon H. Borglum, Sculptor, 1868-1922.*]

"Nebraska Sculptor of the West in World's Fair Equine Sculpture," *World Herald,* Nov. 29, 1903. [See *Highlights in the Life of Solon H. Borglum, Sculptor, 1868-1922.*]

Nelson, Belind. "Life on Cairo Ranch Helped Turn Solon Borglum to Sculpting," *Grand Island Daily Independent*, December 9, 1982.

Opitz, Glenn B. ed. "Solon Hannibal Borglum." *Dictionary of American Sculptors.* Apollo, 1984. p. 42.

Perry, Robert. *Sheep King: The Story of Robert Taylor*. Grand Island, NE: Prairie Pioneer Press and Stuhr Museum of the Prairie Pioneer, 1986.

Price, Willadene. *Gutzon Borglum: The Man Who Carved a Mountain*. N.P., 1961.

"Remarkable Success of an Omaha Sculptor," Omaha 1899. [See *Highlights in the Life of Solon H. Borglum, Sculptor, 1868-1922.*]

"Reproductions of a Selection of the Sculptures of Solon H. Borglum." [See *Highlights in the Life of Solon H. Borglum, Sculptor, 1868-1922.*]

Riedy, Jo, and Ken Harders. *Cairo: A History of the People and the Land (The Early Settlement of Northwest Hall County [Nebraska]).* DVD. 2009.

"A Sculptor of Cowboys," *New York Herald,* June 28, 1903, p. 8. [See *Highlights in the Life of Solon H. Borglum, Sculptor, 1868-1922.*]

Shaff, Howard and Audrey Karl Shaff. *Six Wars At a Time: The Life and Times of Gutzon Borglum, Sculptor of Mount Rushmore*. Sioux Falls, SD: The Center for Western Studies, Augustana College, 1985.

Sklenar, Sherri L. "Paths to Zion: The Mormon Settlement at Wyoming, NE (2010). *Nebraska Anthropologist*. Paper 61. Available at http://digitalcommons.unl.ed/nebanthro/61

"Solon Borglum, the Sculptor, Once a Cowboy," *The Sun*, Oct. 27, 1912, p. 11. [See *Highlights in the Life of Solon H. Borglum, Sculptor, 1868-1922.*]

"Solon Borglum Dies Following Operation: Noted Sculptor and Former Nebraskan Is Victim of Appendicitis: Relatives Live Here," *Omaha World Herald,* Feb. 1, 1922. [See *Highlights in the Life of Solon H. Borglum, Sculptor, 1868-1922.*]

"Solon H. Borglum Dies after Operation," *The New York Times*, January 31, 1922, p. 12.

"Solon Hannibal Borglum," *American National Biography*, Vol. 3. Oxford University Press, 1999. pp. 216-217.

"Solon Hannibal Borglum," *Dictionary of American Biography*, Vol. 2, 1929. p. 462.

"Solon Hannibal Borglum." *The National Cyclopedia of American Biography*. Vol. 13. 1906. p. 214.

Sonne, Conway B. *Ships, Saints, & Mariners - A Maritime Encyclopedia of Mormon Migration 1830-1890,* N.P.: Sonne, 1987. http://freepages.genealogy.rootsweb.ancestry.com/~dianned/monarch_sea.html and http://user.xmission.com/~nelsonb/ship_desc.htm#monarch.

Stange, Pearl. "Wanted to Forget Sod House: Kyhn's (Kyne's) Bluff Inspired Rushmore Genius?" *Grand Island Independent*, Nov 5, 1963 (clipping from the Cairo Roots Museum archives).

Taliaferro, John. *Great White Fathers: The Story of the Obsessive Quest to Create Mount Rushmore*. NY: Public Affairs, 2002.

Wadsworth, Erick L. *The 1866 Mormon Migration* (Master's Thesis). Kearney, Nebraska: University of Nebraska at Kearney, March 2014.

Glossary and Index

Endnotes

[1] Nelson; Stange.
[2] The Morrill Anti-Bigamy Act was passed in 1862.
[3] "Solon Hannibal Borglum," *Dictionary of American Biography*, 462.
[4] Casey and Borglum, 25; Davies, 15," *Dictionary of American Biography*, 462.
[5] Casey and Borglum, 25; Davies, 15.
[6] Shaff, 9-10.
[7] Wadsworth, 22, 42.
[8] Shaff, 9.
[9] Davies, 17.
[10] Shaff, 10.
[11] Davies, 17; Shaff, 915; Wadsworth, 26.
[12] Shaff, 10-11.
[13] Davies, 17; Shaff, 10-11.
[14] Wadsworth, 29.
[15] Breinholt; Carter.
[16] Sonne.
[17] Sonne.
[18] *1864 Emigration.*
[19] *1864 Emigration.*
[20] Email notes from Will Bagley, March 24, 2015.
[21] Bagley, *South Pass*, Chapter 7, pp. 163-200.
[22] Email notes from Will Bagley, March 24, 2015.
[23] Wadsworth, 5, 75-76, 78, 113.
[24] Email notes from Will Bagley, March 24, 2015.
[25] *1864 Emigration*; Wadsworth; Sklenar, 97, 99.
[26] Wadsworth, 5, 75-76, 78, 113; Davies, 20.
[27]Davies, 17; *1864 Emigration*; *Mormon Trail.*
[28] *1864 Emigration*; Wadsworth, 5, 100.
[29] *1864 Emigration*
[30] *1864 Emigration*; Wadsworth, 1, 3, 43, 76; also Notes from talking with Will Bagley, noted Mormon historian and expert, during the Western Writers of America conferences in June 2012 and June 2013.
[31] *1864 Emigration.*
[32] Wadsworth, 79-86.
[33] Wadsworth, 83.
[34] *Along Nebraska Pioneer* Trails, 4; "Nebraska City/Ft. Kearney [sic] Cut-Off"; Mapes, 58.
[35] Wadsworth, 83-90, 103.
[36] Wadsworth, 30.
[37] See http://history.lds.org/overlandtravels/companydatelist for 1864 (William B. Preston Company) and 1865 (Miner G. Atwood Company). See possible error of same birthdate for both Ida and Christina Mikkelsen/Borglum.
[38] http://mormonmigration.lib.byu.edu/Search/showDetails/db:MM_MII/

t:account/id:129;https://history.lds.org/overlandtravels/trailExcerptMulti?lang=eng&pioneerId=32729&sourceId=4788.
[39] Shaff, 12.
[40] Shaff, 12.
[41] Shaff, 12.
[42] Shaff, 11-12.
[43] James Borglum gave many of his children classical first and/or middle names, such as Solon Hannibal Borglum. In ancient Greek history, the name Solon was associated with a famous statesman and law-giver. Also in ancient times, Hannibal was the name of a military commander who conquered much of the known world, often using elephants in place of horses in his cavalry.
[44] Ida's boys and Christina's boys were half-brothers or stepbrothers to each other. They had the same father and their mothers were sisters.
[45] Shaff, 17. The census is a federal count and listing of all people living in an area at a specific time. In America, a census is done every year ending in zero. Census records are great resources to use for looking up family records. The Mormon Church, sometimes called the Latter Day Saints or LDS Church, also keeps excellent searchable family records for genealogy or family researchers.
[46] Shaff, 17.
[47] Shaff, 18-19.
[48] Davies, 20-21.
[49] Shaff, 24-25.
[50] Shaff, 19.
[51] Davies, xvi; Shaff, 17-24.
[52] Davies, 12; Shaff, 2.
[53] Casey and Borglum, 36-38; Shaff, 28.
[54] Davies, 21.
[55] April 15, 2014, email from Ken Harders of the Cairo Roots Museum, giving that information and a legal description of the land. According to the Borglum family (phone conversations with the Borglum grandchildren, March and April, 2014) and the Davies book, 22, James Borglum may have later traded his Pasadena (California) ranch for 6,000 acres of unbroken ranch land along the Loup River in Nebraska, but no land record searches have been able to verify such a large purchase of land by Borglum in those four adjoining counties.
[56] Davies, 28. (The 5'6" height note was taken from a copy of Solon's California voter registration form from 1893 or 1894 when he was 24 and living in California with Gutzon and Lisa. The Cairo Roots Museum has a copy of the voter registration form in its collection.)
[57] Davies, 19.
[58] Davies, 24.
[59] Davies, 22. Possibly 6,000 acres—see note 45.
[60] Davies, 27.
[61] [Graff] Nebraska. Our Towns, 133-134; email from Ken Harders, 3/11/2015.
[62] [Graff]; Riedy & Harders.
[63] [Graff]; *Memories of St. Michael, Nebraska, 105*; Riedy & Harders.

[64] [Graff]; Riedy & Harders.
[65] *Memories of St. Michael, Nebraska*, 109.
[66] Perry, 1.
[67] Davies, 22; *Highlights*.
[68] Davies, 27.
[69] Davies, 27.
[70] Davies, 27.
[71] Davies, 29.
[72] In 1986, a hundred years after Solon first came to the ranch, a farmer was working his field 5 or 6 miles south of White Cloud School when he uncovered part of an ancient pre/proto-Pawnee earthlodge, dating to before1300 AD. The author of this book helped work that official archeological dig that was later recovered with soil.
[73] Davies, 26; "Jan 9, 1887."
[74] Davies, 31-33.
[75] Davies, 31-33; Hassrick 35; "Solon Hannibal Borglum," *Dictionary of American Biography*, 464.
[76] http://www.history.com/this-day-in-history/blizzard-brings-tragedy-to-northwest-plains
[77] "Jan 12, 1888."
[78] Davies, 29.
[79] Davies, 35.
[80] [Editorial]; Stange.
[81] "Drake's Account" and "On the Side"; [Editorial]; *Memories of St. Michael,* Nebraska, 3-4; Stange.
[82] *Memories of St. Michael, Nebraska 1886-1986*, 3-4, 103.
[83] Blackman, 336.
[84] Blackman, 336; *Memories of St. Michael, Nebraska,* 3-4, 6.
[85] *Memories of St. Michael, Nebraska*, 3-4, 43-44, 105, also clipping "Legend of the Bluffs,"no masthead, page or date given.
[86] "Legend of the Bluffs" clipping in *Memories of St. Michael, Nebraska*, no masthead, page, or date given.
[87] Memories of St. Michael, 93; also interviews with current residents.
[88] Personal knowledge of the author and interviews with local residents and historians, including Lurlie Campbell in 2014.
[89] Hassrick, 29.
[90] Bartels.
[91] Davis, 34.
[92] Davies, 35-39.
[93] Davies, 39; Hassrick, 29.
[94] Taliaferro, 82.
[95] Davies, 43; Hassrick, 30; "Solon Hannibal Borglum, *Dictionary of American Biography*, 462-463.
[96] Davies, 44-46.
[97] Hassrick, 32.
[98] Davies, 46.
[99] Davies, 117; Taliaferro, 81-82.

[100] Hassrick, 27.
[101] Davies, 55.
[102] Hassrick, 27.
[103] Hassrick, 35.
[104] Davies, 64, 65.
[105] Davies, 66.
[106] Davies, 66.
[107] Davies, 66.
[108] Davies, 66, 68.
[109] Davies, 68.
[110] Davies, 69.
[111] Davies, 69.
[112] Davies, 73; Hassrick, 36-37.
[113] Davies, 69-70; Hassrick, 36-37.
[114] Davies, 70.
[115] Davies, 73.
[116] Davies, 90, 95, 194.
[117] Davies, 79-80.
[118] Hassrick, 33, 35, 39; "Solon Hannibal Borglum," *American National Biography*, 216.
[119] Davies, 88.
[120] Casey and Borglum, 68.
[121] Davies, 80.
[122] Davies, 88.
[123] Davies, 90, 96.
[124] Davies, 90, 92.
[125] Phone interviews with Monica Borglum Davies' daughter Gwyneth Davies, March and April, 2014.
[126] Davies, 129.
[127] Davies, 112, 114
[128] Davies, 8, 66, 112-123.
[129] Davies, 112-116.
[130] Davies, 116-117.
[131] Lamar, 115; Opitz, 42.
[132] Davies, 124-125; Taliaferro, 101-2.
[133] Davies, Chapter X.
[134] Davies, 129-137.
[135] Davies, 130-137.
[136] Davies, 149, 161-162; Hall, pp. 54-78.
[137] Davies, 161-162; Hall, 59
[138] Davies, 149; Hall, 103, 107.
[139] Davies, 151.
[140] Davies, 162.
[141] Davies, 183,
[142] Davies, 198.
[143] Davies, 199.
[144] Davies, 14.

[145] Davies, 201, 204.
[146] "Solon Hannibal Borglum," *Dictionary of American Biography*, 463.
[147] Davies, 206-207.
[148] Davies, 211.
[149] Shaff, 192.
[150] Shaff, 192-193.
[151] Falk, 66; "Solon H. Borglum Dies after Operation," 12.
[152] Shaff, 193.
[153] Hassrick, 53; Shaff, 193-194.
[154] Davies, 230-233; Hassrick, 53.
[155] *Nebraska Hall of Fame.*
[156] Hassrick, 27, 39, 41, 43, 45.
[157] "Drake's Account; "On the Side"; and Stange.

Noteworthy Americans and Legends of the Plains

Quick Readers Biography Series Books for ages 10-110
and Their National/International Book Awards

Lucky Ears: The True Story of Ben Kuroki, World War II Hero by Jean A. Lukesh, Field Mouse Productions, 2010. *2011 IPPY Bronze Medal Book Award and *2011 Moonbeam Bronze Medal Book Award Winner. (Interest Level: Grade 4 through Adult)

Sky Rider: The Story of Evelyn Sharp, World War II WASP by Jean A. Lukesh, Field Mouse Productions, 2011. (Interest Level: Grades 4/5 through Adult)

Wolves in Blue: Stories of the North Brothers and Their Pawnee Scouts by Jean A. Lukesh, Field Mouse Productions, 2011. *2012 Benjamin Franklin Finalist Silver Medal Book Award Winner and *2012 Western Writers of America SPUR Finalist Book Award. (Interest Level: Grade 7 through Adult)

Eagle of Delight: Portrait of the Plains Indian Girl in the White House by Jean A. Lukesh, Field Mouse Productions, 2013. *2013 Moonbeam Gold Medal; *2013 Literary Classic Gold Medal; *2013 Lumen Gold Award; 2013 Foreword Reviews Magazine's Book of the Year Finalist and Honorable Mention for Children's Nonfiction; 2013 Foreword Reviews Magazine's Book of the Year Finalist for Young Adult Nonfiction; 2013 USA Book Finalist Award; 2014 Benjamin Franklin Finalist Silver Medal Award; *2014 Western Writers of America SPUR Award. (Interest Level: Grades 6 through Adult)

New!!
Secret Brother: The Story of Solon Borglum, "Sculptor of the Prairie" by Jean A. Lukesh, Field Mouse Productions, 2015. (Interest Level: Grade 6/7 through Adult) ***Secret Brother*** is the quick-reading biography of Solon Borglum—the most-secret son of 1860s Mormon immigrants from Denmark. Solon grew up to be a highly regarded Nebraska cowboy, rancher, and sheriff; an early Boy Scout leader, an art instructor, and a decorated World War I hero; and the award-winning world-famous artist known as the "Sculptor of the Prairie." The huge Plains Indian sculptures Solon carved into the Nebraska sandhills near his ranch probably inspired his older and more famous brother (John) Gutzon Borglum to carve his own sculptures of American presidents on Mount Rushmore years later. (Interest level: Young Adult Readers grades 6/7 through adult or ages 13 to 100+)

About the Author
(Dr.) Jean A. Lukesh

Career: Author, Editor, Publisher, Educator, Presenter, Historian, Columnist; Formerly an Educator: Public School Librarian, Media Specialist, Teacher (30 years; now retired)

Education:
B.A. Ed. (Magna cum Laude; Endorsements: Middle School - Language Arts, Social Sciences, General Science; K-12 Educational Media), M.A.Ed. (English); M.A.Ed. (History), Ed.D. (Curriculum & Instruction); Certificate (Publishing).

Author of several books, numerous magazine and newspaper articles and columns, including "The Nebraska Trivia Quiz" in *Nebraska Life Magazine*

Selected Honors:
15 National/International Book Awards
3 State and Regional Book Awards
Nebraska Library Association's Mari Sandoz Award
Mountain/Plains Library Association's Literary Contributions Award
International Reading Association's and Central Nebraska Reading Council's Celebrate Literacy Award
Smithsonian's Community Discovered Trailblazer Award

For more information on Dr. Jean A. Lukesh or her books, see our website at
www.fieldmousebooks.com or
www.fieldmouseproductions.com
Or see her author page at Amazon.com

www.ingramcontent.com/pod-product-compliance
Lightning Source LLC
La Vergne TN
LVHW010656110826
845149LV00014B/3122

* 9 7 8 0 9 8 8 8 0 2 1 3 1 *